GRILLED
PIZZAS
& PIADINAS

GRILLED
PIZZAS
& PIADINAS

CRAIG W. PRIEBE with DIANNE JACOB

PHOTOGRAPHY BY

CHARLES SCHILLER

LONDON, NEW YORK, MELBOURNE,
MUNICH, AND DELHI

EDITOR Anja Schmidt
MANAGING ART EDITOR Michelle Baxter
ART DIRECTOR Dirk Kaufman
DTP COORDINATOR Kathy Farias
PRODUCTION MANAGER Ivor Parker
EXECUTIVE MANAGING EDITOR Sharon Lucas

PHOTOGRAPHY Charles Schiller
FOOD STYLING Susan Vajaranant
PROP STYLING Pamela Duncan Silver

First American Edition, 2008

Published in the United States by
DK Publishing
375 Hudson Street
New York, New York 10014

08 09 10 11 10 9 8 7 6 5 4 3 2 1

GD092 May 2008

A catalog record for this book is available from the
Library of Congress.
ISBN 978-0-7566-3679-1

DK books are available at special discounts when purchased
in bulk for sales promotions, premiums, fund-raising, or
educational use. For details, contact:
DK Publishing Special Markets, 375 Hudson Street, New York,
New York 10014 or SpecialSales@dk.com.

Color reproduction by Colourscan (Singapore)
Printed and bound in China by Leo Paper
Discover more at **www.dk.com**

Contents

Introduction
How I Became Obsessed with Grilled Pizza

In the 1990s I was a young sous chef at an Atlanta hotel kitchen, hard working yet rebellious, longing to do greater things. A sous chef is "one who is under the executive chef." I was tired of being "under" anyone.

One day a beautiful waitress walked into the kitchen. She had long black hair with a streak of silver that outlined her smooth Mediterranean skin. She ignored me for the longest time. When she finally spoke to me, she made me nervous, with her edgy attitude and her big brown eyes.

Eventually, I got the nerve to ask her out. We talked about our dreams and found out how much we had in common. We both loved the restaurant business, and we both wanted to own our own place.

Karla had managed an Italian restaurant for years in St. Louis before coming to Atlanta. I had been cooking in a kitchen since I was a kid, learning things like how to roll ravioli from my Italian grandma. After studying the culinary arts in college, I apprenticed at a classy hotel and went on to travel around the United States, working as a chef in some of the country's best hotels and restaurants.

Karla and I eventually moved in together, and she kept me motivated toward our goal by taking me to business classes. We looked at countless properties for sale or rent, but we didn't have a dime between us.

The Idea Hatches

One day Karla said, "I've got it! We're gonna open a grilled pizza restaurant!" She had read about cooking pizza on a grill somewhere. I wasn't excited. I was trained to prepare anything. Why limit myself to a pizza?

But she was so adamant that I thought I had better make her one. I put together a dough and made a fresh sauce with tomatoes, basil, and garlic. I prepared roasted peppers, prosciutto, caramelized onions, Italian sausage, Gorgonzola cheese, toasted walnuts, and sun-dried tomatoes for the toppings. I didn't want to disappoint her.

We arrived at our apartment after midnight. I fired up our little Smokey Joe grill and rolled out the dough. Once the coals were ready, I tossed the dough onto the grate. The fire came up immediately and singed the hair off my arm. After I finished my little dance, I found out that the fire was too hot and I used too much oil, a volatile combination.

But Karla was going to have her grilled pizza. When I tried again, I tossed the dough onto the grill and watched a network of bubbles rise on the surface. We topped our first grilled pizza and set it under the broiler to crisp. We knew we had found our ticket, even before we tasted it.

Karla and I began grilling pizza almost every night. I liked everything. Karla didn't. But if she slammed her chest with one hand, waved the other one, and shouted, "Oh my God, this is it, Baby!" we knew we had a winner.

The testing process went on for almost a year. Meanwhile we scraped together $100,000 in credit at an outrageous interest rate. Not long after, we saw a "pizza pie" business for sale in the classified ads. With the stroke of a pen, an 800-square-foot filthy takeout—with broken refrigeration and no air conditioning—was ours. To celebrate, Karla and I got married.

C.K.'s Grilled Pizza Debuts

On the first night we took ownership of the restaurant, we were on our hands and knees, scrubbing stains off the tile floor. Eventually, a fresh coat of paint, latticework, potted plants, and a new chalkboard menu gave the place a cute homemade look. My mom, an accomplished painter, splashed murals of the Italian countryside on the walls, giving the place an artsy appeal.

The shop had a stone deck oven for regular pizzas, so we started out making those. With no indoor grilling equipment, however, we couldn't move forward with the grilled versions that we worked so hard on. A friend suggested that we fire up a grill in the alley. I put our old Weber around the back and added grilled pizza titles to the menu.

When customers ordered a grilled pizza, they watched me roll out the dough, take it down the hall, and step out the back door. I reappeared with a grilled crust, added the toppings, and disappeared out the back door

again. About eight minutes later I came back with a fully cooked pizza.

For multiple orders, people waited up to an hour to get irregularly shaped pizzas full of bumpy ridges and pockets of flavor. That was part of their unique charm. Some folks just didn't get it but, fortunately, lots of others did.

C.K.'s (Craig and Karla's) Grilled Pizza lasted five years and expanded to a full-service restaurant for two more. My pizzas went on to win culinary awards. *Pizza Today* named our place one of "the Nation's Top 100 Pizzerias" for five years in a row. The *Atlanta Journal-Constitution* listed it on the city's annual "Top 50 Restaurants" list. *Travel + Leisure* wrote a piece listing the best six pizzerias in America, including ours.

Moving On

At the end of seven years, we had two kids and we were tired. After Karla was robbed at knifepoint while delivering a pizza, we moved to Chicago, my hometown. I answered an ad to become a private chef for a multibillion dollar investment firm, the Henry Crown Company. Now I make meals at the office for the Crown family and their guests, who include diplomats, politicians, CEOs, and other well-connected folks. Karla stays home with our two children.

I still make my grilled pizzas for lunches, dinners, and catered events. I hope you enjoy them as much as Karla does, and she's still a tough critic.

How to Use This Book

The surest way to success is to prepare all the ingredients before putting the dough on the fire. That's how my restaurant worked. By the time we opened for the day, we had already grilled crusts, sausages, chicken breasts, and peppers, and prepared sautéed mushrooms, shredded cheese, and sauces. A four-foot stack of grilled crusts sat on the counter. That way, when customers ordered, I scooped the prepared ingredients out of bowls and got them onto the crusts quickly.

Save time

The recipes in this book suggest ways to prepare in advance. To cut down further on time, you may want to buy some ingredients instead of making them yourself, such as pre-made crusts, grilled chicken, pesto, and roasted peppers.

The salad bars at grocery stores can be a bonanza when you need a ¼ cup or ½ cup of something. I get small amounts of sun-dried tomatoes, cut-up cantaloupe, olives, and roasted peppers there.

Another timesaver is to make bigger quantities of sauces and toppings and to freeze them for individual use. That way they will be ready whenever you are. Chapter 3 covers the toppings I use most and how to store them.

Stock your pantry

By keeping the following items stocked in your kitchen, you are prepared at all times for grilled pizza. Party shopping becomes much easier, as you will need fewer ingredients.

Here is a list of essentials and their shelf life. Keep all sealed in airtight canisters in your pantry, unless otherwise indicated.

- Unbleached flour: 6 months
- Whole wheat flour: 6 months
- Cornmeal: 3 months
- Sugar: 6 months
- Yeast: Keep refrigerated for 6 months
- Salt: 12 months
- Extra virgin olive oil: 6 months
- Parmesan cheese: Keep in the freezer for 3 months
- Mozzarella cheese: Keep in the freezer for 3 months, or in the refrigerator for 2 weeks
- Dry herbs: 3 months
- Garlic: Keep refrigerated for 1 month
- Charcoal or wood for grills: These items keep indefinitely in dry storage. Have lots on hand whenever the urge to light your fire strikes.

General Guidelines on Making Pizza

Some pizzas in this book are more ambitious than others, particularly the award-winners (these will be pointed out in their headnotes). The payoff, however, is worth it. The deep flavors and variety of textures create pizzas unlike any you've eaten before.

Pizza basics

All pizza recipes call for a 12-inch crust with one grilled side. You'll roll out the dough and slide it onto the grill for 2 to 3 minutes. Then remove the crust, flip it over, and brush the grilled side of the crust with Herbed Grill Oil (page 28), extra virgin olive oil, or melted butter.

Next comes the creative part: layering toppings. All toppings should be placed out to the edge of the pizza, because it has no rim. When you build your pizzas, don't pile all the ingredients on in layers. Instead, go for an artistic mosaic pattern. The pizza should have a different taste in each bite. It should not be loaded, because a heavy pizza is harder to maneuver on the grill, to cut, and to eat. Plus, it tastes the same in every bite.

Once the toppings are on the pizza, it goes back on the grill for a few minutes. The ingredients are already cooked, so it's a matter of crisping the crust and heating the toppings. A short visit in your oven's broiler also cooks the top, creates a crisp, brown topping, and caramelizes the sauces.

Piadinas

About a quarter of this book is dedicated to grilled piadinas, folded Italian sandwiches that resemble flour tortillas, but are more tender. Piadina dough needs only a 30-minute rest to relax the glutens in the flour. The rounds are best when grilled just before filling them with meats, cheeses, and roasted vegetables.

Desserts

If you're looking for something new and surprising to serve your friends, see Chapter 11. While restaurants have been serving dessert pizzas for years, it's still a novelty to have them at home. I first used my grilled pizza crust as a dessert on the recommendation of a loyal patron, who bought some of my plain grilled crusts. He said that he buttered them and sprinkled them with sugar, then ate them with fruit pie filling or with ice cream.

I was amazed that anyone would buy a plain pizza crust for dessert. He sparked my curiosity, so I tried it. I buttered and sugared a grilled crust just as he described. It was fantastic: flaky, tender, sweet, and lightly smoky. The smoky part may sound a little different, but it adds a great dimension as a cookie. Try a few and you'll see what I mean.

You'll be surprised by how few tools you need to grill a pizza. This chapter starts with an overview of outdoor grills, both charcoal and gas. If you don't have one of these, you don't have to run out and buy one, because next I'll cover all the indoor grills, griddles, and skillets that work just as well. Finally, I'll discuss a few essential tools for the grill and kitchen, and some that are nice to have.

Grills &
Gadgets

Outdoor Grills

The fresh air whirling around the fire, a seasoned grill, and the smoky charcoal combine to give grilled pizzas and piadinas deeper flavors and a gratifying crispness you can't get indoors. Friends and family are always drawn to the flame.

Charcoal grills

Charcoal grills are my first choice for grilling pizza, because nothing beats the flavor of cooking over a natural fire. The grilling surface must be large enough to accommodate my standard 12-inch (30 cm) pizza, or 10 inches (25 cm) at the smallest. I have made pizzas on charcoal grills ranging from $6 to $1000, and my favorite is the kettle style, such as a Weber (A). But a hibachi (B) works well too.

One environmental note: Grillers in the United States use an estimated 46,250 tons of charcoal lighter fluid each year. Please do not increase this number by using lighter fluid to start your charcoal. Lighter fluid is made entirely of volatile organic compounds that help form ozone, which contributes to global warming and other pollution-related issues.

Besides, lighter fluid tends to add a bitter taste to grilled foods because of the organic compounds in the smoke. And over time, the lighter fluid impregnates the ceramic or metal coating of your grill. The compounds will never burn off and pollute the food you grill. You may not realize this until you compare food cooked with lighter fluid and without it. Use a metal chimney instead (see page 17). It costs the same as a couple of cans of lighter fluid. It will pay for itself in a few months, last for 5 years, and will give you a professional, consistent result every time. I also recommend using natural wood charcoal versus briquettes as they give a smoother burn. For more convincing, see the box on page 17.

Gas grills

A gas grill (C) provides consistent, readily available grilling because it's so easy to start a fire and control it. I use mine when it's raining and I don't want to hang around outside. The only drawbacks are that gas grills generally do not burn as hot as a natural fire, and some flavor is sacrificed with the lack of charcoal or wood. Typically, gas grills have ceramic briquettes or lava rocks, heated by gas jets. They heat up quickly, in as little as 5 minutes. Look for a grill with up to 45,000 BTUs.

Caring for your grill

Many cooks think that grease from previous grilling somehow "seasons" the grill or the food. In reality, grilling on a dirty grill is just like frying in a pan with yesterday's eggs stuck to it.

1 Before starting your fire, brush the grill's surface with a copper or steel wire brush. Use a quick forward and backward motion. Push the brush through the grate so that it removes debris between the grooves.

2 Wipe the grate surface with a rag, or use a wad of paper towels. This will remove the finer dust that you stirred up with the brush.

3 To make it easier to move your pizza around, spray your grill's surface with an even coat of nonstick spray. You could also wipe the surface with paper towels moistened with vegetable oil, but nonstick spray is easier and gives a consistently even coat.

4 Repeat steps 1 through 3 once or twice more to ensure all the dirt is removed.

5 After you have started your fire and your grill is hot, give the surface one more spray or wipe.

6 When you're done cooking, give the cooling grill a quick brush. Debris comes off a grill more easily when it is still hot.

Regular maintenance: Every couple of weeks, dip your grill brush in soapy water and scrub the grate. Follow with a light coat of nonstick spray to keep it from rusting. Proper maintenance extends the life of your grill.

A

B

C

Indoor Grills

Sometimes an outdoor grill is not an option, particularly if you live in an apartment without a balcony or backyard. This does not mean that you cannot grill a terrific pizza. Many different types of indoor grills do a remarkable job.

Built-in gas or electric grills

Some homes have built-in grills in the kitchen. The gas burners usually grill every bit as well as the larger outdoor grills. Sometimes they are a little narrow, because they are designed to grill meats primarily, but most are at least 10 inches across, and that's just right for a pizza. Built-in electric grills must be powered by at least 2500 watts to be effective.

Cast-iron grill pans

These pans (A) have raised ridges that leave grill marks on food. A thin crust gets crispy in a couple of minutes when you put the pan on high heat. They take a little longer to heat, about 10 minutes, but retain their temperature better than other metal pans. See pages 42–43 for grilling instructions.

Cast-iron skillet

Same pan, no raised ridges.

Skillets or frying pans

Like grill pans, a thin crust gets crispy in a couple of minutes when you put it on high heat in a skillet. Choose one large enough to accommodate a 10- to 12-inch (25 to 30 cm) pizza.

Flat griddles

These solid surface grilling appliances (B) are sometimes built into stovetops. Their original intent is for griddling pancakes, searing meats, and frying eggs. If a griddle can make a pancake, it can grill a pizza. I've tried it. See pages 44–45 for grilling instructions.

Panini grills

These are similar to contact grill presses (see opposite page), except that the lid is often heavier (C). Panini grills have ample wattage for serious crisping power. The best wattage is 1500 BTUs.

A

B

Contact grill presses

(Also called a clamshell or a George Foreman.) This grill press (D) makes surprisingly good pizza crusts. It cooks both sides at the same time, creating a crisp crust right on your countertop. I didn't believe it until I tried it myself. The best wattage is 1000 to 1500. See pages 46–47 for grilling instructions.

Open-faced electric grills

This stand-alone appliance (E) is designed to grill like an outdoor grill because of its flat, open, cast-aluminum grooved surface. It also creates particularly good grill marks on your crust if you're willing to wait twice as long to get it crisp. Costing anywhere from $39 to $200, most electric grills are about $70. The less expensive ones work just as well as the heavy hitters, but might only fit 10-inch (25 cm) pizzas instead of 12-inch (30 cm) ones.

The most important aspect of this grill is its wattage. You need at least 1500 watts. Anything less just won't do the job because it won't be hot enough. Check the bottom of the appliance for the information.

If your grill has an adjustable thermostat, you won't need it. Keep the temperature at its highest setting throughout.

When purchasing one of these grills, look for an easy-to-clean cooking surface. Oxidized aluminum or stainless steel is best. Beware of the cheaper grills with nonstick surfaces, as the nonstick coating can flake off and end up on your food. I'd avoid them altogether.

Tuscan grills

(Also called fireplace or hearth grills.) This recreational way of grilling is making a comeback. Grilling pizza on the hearth gives the crust an amazingly smoky flavor because the wood has been seasoned and not burned. And it's fun to do.

Designed specifically for fireplaces, Tuscan grills (F) are usually made from cast iron for the best heat conduction. They cost anywhere from $49 to $200, depending upon their size and features. The grill is a grid with four legs that you place over a fire, once the flame has burned down to hot embers (see page 47 for preparing a Tuscan grill for use).

You'll need a few extra tools, such as a spit-type poker to move the hot logs, and a small fireplace shovel for gathering the embers. Otherwise, follow the instructions on pages 38–41 for outdoor grilling.

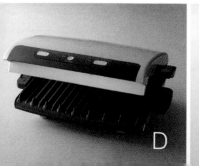

D   E   F

Grilling Tools

Having the right gear makes your job easier in the kitchen and out on the grill. You'll find you need surprisingly few tools. If you're like me, you like to start with the essentials. Once I get comfortable, I expand my tool collection to a few more items that make sense. Read the following to get started on the necessities and extras.

Long-handled tongs

To keep my hands away from the fire, I like stainless-steel tongs at least 14 to 16 inches long (A). These are indispensable for gripping and maneuvering pizza crust on a hot grill.

The secret is to move the tongs into the center of the crust first, before moving it, instead of grabbing the pizza on the edges and trying to pull it, which can rip the edges off the pizza. You'll be surprised by how easily the pizza moves when half of it rests on the tongs.

It's tempting to use a spatula instead. But I find that a spatula does not give me the control required to handle a 12-inch pizza crust on a hot grill. But then again, some people swear by it and wouldn't use anything else.

Extra-long oven mitts

Protect your hands when using the grill. Heavy-duty, long mitts (B) are best.

Wire brush

You need a good grill brush (C) for cleaning your grill. Get a brush with a comfortable handle at least 18 inches long to keep your hands away from the hot scrubbing, and to get the leverage you need to brush off charred food. The kind I like has an 8-inch head, perpendicular to the handle, with brass and stainless-steel bristles that will not rust. Keeping your grill clean will keep your pizza crust clean, and can add years to the life of your grill (see page 13 for cleaning instructions).

Pizza screen

These round stainless-steel, or aluminum, disks are made of either a heavy mesh screen or heavier perforated steel (D–E). They come in diameters ranging from 8 to 18 inches, and are available at most culinary stores and food-service supply shops.

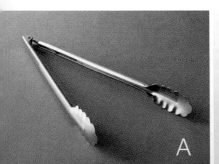

A

B

C

Placing your dough on a screen prevents it from tearing or sticking because you don't lift the crust directly from the grill. The screen supports the dough beautifully, even buffering the heat if the grill gets too hot. Plus, it's easier to move the pizza around, because you move the screen, rather than the pizza.

Wood chips

I often use wood chips to add flavor to my grilled foods, particularly if I'm grilling on a gas grill, which loses some of the flavor of natural fire. I make a small foil packet of wood chips soaked in water, and set it on the burner. The smoke comes up through the pizza dough and adds a subtle, smoky flavor. My favorite types of wood are hickory, alder, cherry, and maple.

Coal chimney

This cylindrical metal can (F) is the best way to start your fire without lighter fluid. Any hardware or culinary store stocks them. See the box at right to decide what kind of charcoal to use.

NATURAL WOOD CHARCOAL VERSUS BRIQUETTES

Natural wood (also called lump or chunk hardwood) charcoal is wood that has been burned to remove its resins. The result is a smooth, even burn for your grill. Here's why I prefer them to briquettes:

• Charcoal briquettes need petroleum by-products to hold them together. Natural wood is virtually free of tars that can contain carcinogenic compounds.

• Natural wood charcoal burns with an aroma that scents your dough as it grills. Briquettes don't do that.

• Natural wood burns with a more even heat distribution than charcoal briquettes, giving you a more consistent cooking surface.

• Natural wood burns hotter and faster than briquettes. Your fire will be ready in half the time.

• It takes more briquettes to reach higher temperatures than natural wood charcoal.

• Natural wood keeps your grill cleaner because it has a much lower ash production than briquettes.

Look for 20- to 40-pound (13½ to 18 kg) bags at home improvement stores, hardware stores, grocery stores, and warehouse clubs.

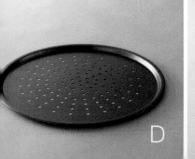

D

E

F

Kitchen Tools

Over time, I've learned that some tools do a better job. The differences might be subtle, but they affect the quality of the finished product. I use all of the following tools, because when I make lots of pizzas, efficiency is important.

Rolling pin

The best rolling pins are made of solid wood and have tapered ends. These are called French rolling pins (A). The tapered ends help you get an even pressure across the whole pin when rolling out the dough. Get one that is about 20 inches (50 cm) long. This size will allow easy maneuverability when you are rolling out 12-inch (30 cm) diameter circles.

Pastry brush

A brush comes in handy to paint tasty olive oil or melted butter on your crust. I like small paintbrushes with a 6-inch (15 cm), heat-resistant plastic or wooden handle. Mine has sterilized natural bristles 1½ to 2 inches (3 to 5 cm) wide. Less expensive brushes come with synthetic bristles, often made of nylon, but natural bristles hold more liquid and will not melt upon contact with a hot surface.

Buy a food-grade pastry brush instead of regular hardware-type paintbrushes.

Paintbrushes may be treated with inedible compounds or chemicals that can contaminate your food. Since they are not meant for food service, they will rust and lose their bristles more quickly than the tightly bound bristles on food-service brushes.

When I'm in someone else's kitchen and can't find a brush, I use a wad of paper towels.

A decent knife

I prefer a knife with a handle that has a solid piece of steel running all the way through it for full strength. The best knives are made from high carbon stainless steel with high chromium content. These blades are extremely resistant to pitting, breaking, or rusting. The handle should be ergonomically constructed from wood or polypropylene, with no exposed rivets.

Henckel or Wüsthof Trident knives are two of the best. A quality knife might cost $75 to $125, but should provide a lifetime of good service in the kitchen.

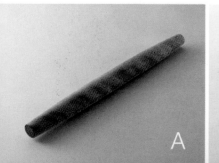

A

B

If you only buy one good knife, get an 8- to 10-inch (20 to 25 cm) chef's knife. This is a normal kitchen knife with a pointed tip, a straight blade and back, and a bolster or balance point to prevent your fingers from slipping onto the blade. These knives are great for just about every kitchen prep task.

Measuring cups

To use dry measuring cups correctly, use another cup to scoop up a dry ingredient such as flour. Fill the cup to the brim, then sweep off the excess with a knife to create a level amount.

When using a liquid measuring cup, place the cup on a level surface and fill it with liquid to the correct fill line. Wait for the liquid to be still, then bring to eye level to make sure the liquid is even with the line.

Stand or electric mixer

A stand mixer takes the hard work out of mixing and kneading pizza dough. Kitchen-Aid manufactures great mixers—I wouldn't be without mine. Always use the dough blade, which is a C- or S-shaped paddle. It slips the dough off and presses down onto the dough as it picks it back up, effectively kneading it to develop the gluten or elasticity in the flour.

Do not use handheld mixers, the ones with two spinning beaters, as they are used to beat semi-solid and liquid ingredients.

Stainless-steel bowls

Mixing dough by hand is best done in a deep stainless-steel bowl. Sauces and toppings stay fresh and taste best when refrigerated or frozen in this type of bowl as well, as it doesn't absorb flavors the way plastic does. The beauty of stainless steel is that you can carry the bowls outdoors to your grilling area and if you drop them, they won't break. It's nice to have a variety of sizes.

Dough blade

A dough blade (B) is a flat 6-inch (15 cm) rectangular scraper that is not sharp. It has a plastic, wooden, or stainless-steel handle on top, rather than on the side. I use this tool for cutting dough and picking excess flour and dough off my counter. You can find this tool at most kitchen supply stores.

Pizza cutter

I use a knife to cut pizza, but I also like a rocking pizza cutter with a curved single blade, called a mezzaluna (C). You rock it back and forth over a pizza to separate the pieces. The cutting action is downward. Its advantage is that it cuts the pizza into small pieces without pulling the pizza apart.

Curved pizza cutters have a single blade, unlike the double-blade mezzaluna used primarily to chop herbs. They are sold at finer gourmet stores and stores that sell food-service equipment.

I don't recommend the wheel-blade pizza cutters. This cutter is best for heavier or thicker pizzas, because it pushes through a pizza with a forward motion. You can push a thin, light, and crispy pizza right off the counter with one of these if you're not careful.

The test of a great pizza is its irresistible crust. If you have never had a pizza with a thin grilled crust, you will love its crispy texture and charred flavor. The process for preparing your own dough is easy and flexible. My favorite method is to use a stand mixer. A food processor saves time, however, and kneading by hand can be easy and relaxing. No matter which method you choose, your grilled pizza dough will turn out well if you follow these easy instructions.

Pizza Dough

Basic Grilled Pizza Dough

I prefer using unbleached flour for my pizza dough because bleached flour has chlorine agents that remove nutrients such as beta-carotene from the dough. These natural nutrients add flavor, color, and more nutrition to your pizza crust. A little whole wheat flour results in a more robust and chewy crust. It also makes the dough easier to handle on the grill. Up to 25 percent of the flour could be whole wheat. Any more than that, and the dough becomes too dense, heavy, and won't rise enough. This recipe is easily doubled.

1 Pour the warm water into a small bowl or measuring cup. (If the water is too hot, the yeast will die. If too cold, it will not activate.) Add the yeast and sugar and stir until the yeast dissolves into a smooth beige color. Let it stand on your counter for about 5 minutes to prove that the yeasted water is active. A thin layer of foam will appear at the top, indicating that the batch is good.

2 **Kneading with a stand mixer:** Add the flours, salt, and cornmeal to a 4- or 5-quart (4 or 5 liter) standing mixing bowl. Use the dough hook attachment on the lowest speed to mix the dry ingredients. Add the yeasted water and the 2 tablespoons of olive oil. Mix on the slowest speed to allow the ingredients to come together. You may need to scrape down the sides with a spatula. Then move to medium-high speed and knead for 2 minutes. The batter should form a ball, unless it's too wet or sticky. If so, add only enough flour to prevent it from sticking. The dough should come off the sides cleanly and form a ball.

   Kneading with a food processor: Measure all of the ingredients into the bowl. Use the plastic blade made especially for dough. (The metal blade may tear the dough to pieces.) Use a pulse action until the dough comes together. Continue to pulse the dough in quick bursts for about 3 minutes. This technique keeps the dough from overheating.

INGREDIENTS

¾ cup warm water

1 packet active dry yeast (about 2¼ teaspoons)

½ teaspoon sugar

1½ cups unbleached flour

¼ cup whole wheat flour

1 teaspoon kosher salt

2 tablespoons cornmeal, preferably white, plus additional for the pan

2 tablespoons extra virgin olive oil, plus ¼ teaspoon for the bowl

Makes two 12-inch (30 cm) pizzas

Thicker Crust Variation
Stir 1½ tablespoons dry milk powder into the yeasted water. Adding dry milk powder creates a thick crust, more like those served at traditional pizza parlors. This Sicilian-style crust has a crisp outer layer when grilled, and will be softer than the thin-crust version. When you grill thicker dough, use a slightly cooler fire, and grill for a few minutes longer. This way the outer crust does not burn before the middle of the dough cooks through.

Kneading by hand: Measure the flours, salt, and cornmeal into a large bowl. Add the yeasted water and the 2 tablespoons of olive oil. Mix well, stirring with a strong spoon. Lightly flour a clean, dry countertop. Form a ball of dough, place it on the counter, and press down with the palm of your hand. Fold the dough over itself and press again. Continue to roll and press the dough for about 8 minutes until the dough is smooth. (You will feel the dough change. It will soften and become more elastic.) Add only enough flour to prevent it from sticking.

3 Put the remaining ¼ teaspoon of olive oil in a medium bowl. The dough will be sticky, so flour your hands before picking it up, and place it in the bowl. Turn it over several times until it is coated in oil. This prevents a crust from forming on its surface as it rises.

4 Cover with plastic wrap, and place in a draft-free, warm place, 70° to 80°F (20° to 25°C), for 2 hours, until it rises to almost double in appearance.

5 Chill the dough in the refrigerator overnight, or for 1 hour to firm it up. Since this dough is slightly sticky, chilling the dough makes it easier to roll out. Chilling it overnight gives the dough more flavor and texture. Dough will keep in the refrigerator for 3 days.

Note: This recipe makes two crusts. If you're planning to prepare only one pizza, grill the second crust anyway, because it will keep better than dough. Crusts keep in the refrigerator for 3 days, or for up to 3 months in the freezer. Then you'll be ready to grill pizza anytime. You can even cheat by cooking the pizza in the oven. Try 400°F (200°C) for 12 minutes, and check toward the end to avoid burning. Put the frozen crust right onto the grill. It will only take a minute to thaw. Or defrost it in the refrigerator or at room temperature; it will thaw quickly, within a half hour.

SAVE TIME WITH PRE-MADE DOUGH OR CRUSTS

Many customers came into my pizza shop to buy raw dough to grill or bake. Your local pizzeria might also sell dough for this purpose. Trader Joe's sells terrific fresh pizza dough that grills up beautifully. Pillsbury sells decent pizza dough that tastes great grilled.

Frozen bread dough is a little different. It grills more like bread than pizza crust. It chars nicely with grill marks, but comes out softer because it has no cornmeal, and because the ratio of yeast is lower. I have also grilled pita bread, and used it as a small crust for pizza, which works well too. A prepared crust, such as Boboli, works if you grill both sides first to crisp it.

Rolling Out the Dough

Treat your dough gently. Kneading or shaping it into a ball could make it too stiff. Do not roll out your pizza until your grill is almost ready. If the dough sits around on a cookie sheet for just a few minutes, it could become sticky.

1 Your refrigerated dough should have doubled in size. Punch it down gently to remove gas.

2 Lightly flour about a foot of space on a clean, dry countertop. Flatten the dough with your hands to about a 1-inch (2½ cm) thickness. Cut in half with a knife.

3 Put one piece of dough in the center of the floured space and sprinkle a little flour over the top. Using a rolling pin, make smooth strokes to roll out the dough starting from the center out to the edges.

4 Work around the diameter of the dough to form a circular crust with an even thickness. It is not necessary to maintain a perfect circle. Roll the dough out to about a 12-inch (30 cm) diameter, about ⅛ inch thick. Sprinkle the crust with a fine layer of flour. It will make the dough easier to handle, and prevents stickiness.

5 Position 2 cookie sheets with no sides, or 2 pizza screens, next to your dough. (I sometimes use the back of a cookie sheet.) Sprinkle them generously with flour or cornmeal, so the dough will not stick. Pick up the dough with two hands and fold it gently in half.

6 Transfer the dough to a cookie sheet.

7 Unfold the dough onto the pan to make it flat.

8 Stretch out the dough to an approximate 12-inch (30 cm) diameter.

9 Repeat with the second piece of dough on the second cookie sheet.

Note: if you are grilling inside or on a small outside grill, you may need to roll out smaller diameter pizzas to fit your appliance.

A variety of sauces and toppings results in a grilled pizza with layers of flavor and textures. In addition to the vibrant sauces presented here, I've found that roasting, grilling, or toasting raw ingredients such as garlic, mushrooms, nuts, and red peppers brings out more flavor than using them raw. I like to keep these items on hand at all times. At any given moment a sudden urge to have grilled pizza may strike, and I'll be ready.

Sauces
& Toppings

The Building Blocks

Herbed Grill Oil

I use this oil as a base for almost all of my savory pizzas and many of the piadinas. It takes just a second to make and keeps in the refrigerator indefinitely. If I'm feeling lazy, sometimes I add a little more olive oil instead of making a new batch. Make sure the olive oil is top quality.

INGREDIENTS

½ cup extra virgin olive oil

1 small clove garlic, minced

½ teaspoon dried oregano

½ teaspoon dried thyme

½ teaspoon dried basil

Makes ½ cup

Place all of the ingredients in a small bowl or glass jar, mix well, and refrigerate. If it solidifies, take it out a few minutes early or microwave it at 5-second intervals until it starts to liquefy.

USES FOR LEFTOVER HERBED GRILL OIL:

As a marinade for meats, poultry, seafood, or vegetables.

Sauté vegetables, shrimp, chicken, or tofu in it.

Mix it with a little vinegar, salt, and pepper for a salad dressing.

Stir it into hot pasta and add cheese.

Brush it on grilled bread or toast to make bruschetta.

Toss it with potatoes, then season it with salt and pepper and roast.

Chunky Tomato Basil Sauce

This vibrant, fresh sauce is so much better than anything from a jar. The tomatoes are roughly chopped, rather than puréed, so the sauce sits on top of the pizza rather than underneath the toppings. This way you don't get the same taste in every bite. Tomato paste deepens the sauce's flavor, as does refrigerating the sauce for at least an hour. If your tomatoes are juicy, use more tomato paste to thicken the sauce. This sauce keeps in the refrigerator for 3 days.

INGREDIENTS

2 small cloves garlic

8 large fresh basil leaves

1½ pounds (about 3 medium) ripe tomatoes, cored and quartered (see Note)

2 tablespoons tomato paste (or more)

1 teaspoon kosher salt

¾ teaspoon freshly ground black pepper

½ teaspoon sugar

Note: If tomatoes are not in season, use good canned tomatoes instead. They will have more flavor than the gas-ripened ones at the supermarket. Use two 14½-ounce (440 g) cans of diced tomatoes, drained.

Makes about 2 cups, depending on ripeness and juiciness

1 Place the garlic and basil leaves in a food processor and pulse until finely chopped. Add the tomatoes and pulse briefly. Do not purée the tomatoes, as the sauce is meant to be chunky. Or chop all by hand.

2 Transfer to a medium bowl. Stir in the tomato paste, salt, pepper, and sugar until mixed well. If the sauce looks watery, add more tomato paste until you see no more juice.

3 Refrigerate the sauce for an hour to accentuate the flavors.

Grilled Chicken Breast

Boneless, skinless chicken breasts are easy, fast, and a no-waste product. Fresh is best but the frozen ones are convenient because you can take out just one breast at a time, defrost it, and throw it on the grill. To defrost, leave it in your refrigerator overnight, or place in a colander in the sink, and run cool water over it for 10 minutes. I like to grill four at a time, tear them into bite-sized chunks, and freeze them in individual bags so they're ready for topping a pizza or slipping into a piadina. They'll last for up to 1 month.

To save time: Many grocery stores sell pre-made grilled chicken in the deli case, or in small packs next to salad lettuces or processed meats, already cut up.

INGREDIENTS

One 6-ounce (175 g) boneless, skinless chicken breast

1 teaspoon extra virgin olive oil or Herbed Grill Oil (page 28)

$1/8$ teaspoon salt

¼ teaspoon freshly ground black pepper

1 Place the chicken breast in a shallow container. Sprinkle with the oil, salt, and pepper and rub into the meat, distributing them evenly.

2 Grill the breast over the hottest part of a medium-high fire for about 10 minutes, depending on the thickness of the breast. Turn it once or twice.

3 The meat is done when the juice runs clear when pierced with a knife tip. Do not overcook or the breast will dry out. If you have a thermometer, grill the breast to an internal temperature of 165°F (75°C).

Toasted Nuts

It only takes a moment to toast nuts, and you will be surprised by how their flavor deepens. Freeze them for up to 3 months in a tightly sealed plastic freezer bag.

1 Heat a dry skillet over medium heat. Add the amount of nuts your recipe calls for and shake the pan. After 1 minute the nuts will crackle. Toss them around in the pan until you notice a slight change in color to golden brown.

2 When you smell their aroma, they're done. The whole process takes only 2 to 3 minutes. Do not walk away. They will burn fast.

3 Transfer to a plate and cool for a few moments before applying them to the pizza, piadina, or salad of your choice.

Basil Pecan Pesto

Pesto is attributed to the Ligurian region of northern Italy. Originally, pesto sauce had no basil. Instead, cheese, olive oil, and pine nuts were blended to form a thick paste. Since the Genovese hills were abundant with wild basil, cooks added it to the blend later, much to everyone's delight. This sauce became known as Pesto alla Genovese. The pesto-based pizzas at my restaurant were always popular, perhaps because my sauce is a little different than the traditional kind. I use roasted pecans instead of pine nuts to give this pesto a robust, earthy taste. Italian parsley and onion add even more flavor. I like to make pesto in bulk and freeze it in flat, round, clear deli containers. That way they stack well. When wrapped in plastic until tightly sealed, they'll last up to 6 months.

To save time: Any quality store-bought pesto will work in the grilled pizza recipes.

USES FOR LEFTOVER BASIL PECAN PESTO:

Thin it with a little water, fruit juice, or beer and use it to baste grilled meats.

Mix it with cream for pasta.

Make the Antipasto Pasta Salad (page 142), the Piadina Genovese (page 126), or the PAT Piadina (page 132).

INGREDIENTS

1 bunch of basil

¼ cup extra virgin olive oil

⅓ cup grated Parmesan

¼ cup roasted pecans

1 clove garlic

¼ cup Italian parsley leaves, lightly packed

1 tablespoon chopped onions

Pinch of black pepper

¼ teaspoon kosher salt

¼ teaspoon sugar

Makes about ¾ cup

1 Grasp the basil bunch and twist to tear off the thick stems. The remainder should measure about 2 cups.

2 Place all of the ingredients in a food processor and process until smooth.

Roasted Red Pepper Strips

These colorful, tasty strips of pepper give many pizzas in this book an instant lift. While I might specify red or green peppers, feel free to use them interchangeably and include yellow, orange, or purple peppers. I like to grill peppers whole for better flavor and texture. The steam inside makes the skins moist, and trapped juices build up the flavor. This recipe can be doubled, tripled, and saved for future pizzas. Roasted peppers will keep in your refrigerator for 2 weeks. Don't put them in the freezer, though, as they will turn to mush.

To save time: Buy bottled roasted peppers. Some stores have deli counters with grilled vegetables, and the counter person can extract a few freshly grilled red peppers for you.

INGREDIENTS

1 red or green bell pepper, washed

½ teaspoon extra virgin olive oil

Pinch of salt

Makes about ½ cup pepper strips

1 *On the barbecue:* If you happen to have a hot grill going, make use of it. Using long-handled tongs, place the pepper on the hottest part of the fire. *Gas stovetop:* This is how I grill peppers most of the time. Turn a stovetop burner to high and place a pepper directly on the flame. *Electric stovetop:* Put the pepper directly on the electric element. *Oven method:* Turn your oven to broil, and place the pepper on an oiled cookie sheet under the broiler.

2 No matter which method you choose, soon you'll hear the pepper crackle, and a toasty aroma will come off the skin. Turn the pepper with tongs to make sure all sides get direct heat, 2 to 3 minutes for each side. Each side must receive the full blast of heat. This will char the entire pepper completely black. That's a good thing.

3 Place the charred pepper in a bowl. Cover with plastic wrap. Let it sit for about 5 minutes, so the steam can loosen the skin and make it easier to peel.

4 Take the pepper to the sink and put a strainer under it before you gently peel off the black skin. Pull off the stem and remove the core and seeds. Give the pepper a *slight* rinse with cool water—some flavor can be washed down the drain if you rinse them completely.

5 If not using immediately, toss in the olive oil and salt, seal in a plastic bag, and refrigerate.

Roasted Garlic Cloves

These little nuggets are like flavor mines. When you find one on a pizza, it fills your mouth with a rich, earthy, sweet taste. Add them to any pizza when you want to boost the flavor. I add water as a roasting tool. The garlic stays soft and buttery, yet still holds its shape when you place it on the pizza. If you roast the cloves in olive oil, they become too crispy and sometimes dry out. To store, leave the cloves in the juice. They will keep for about 2 weeks in your refrigerator.

To save time: Many stores sell peeled fresh garlic cloves. I always look for them before I spend the time to peel garlic. Look in the produce department for small glass or plastic containers. Do not confuse raw cloves with pickled, chopped, or crushed garlic.

INGREDIENTS

12 cloves garlic, peeled

1 teaspoon extra virgin olive oil

Pinch of salt

¾ to 1 cup water
(enough to cover)

Makes 12 cloves garlic, enough for 1 pizza

1 Preheat the oven or toaster oven to 400°F (200°C). Place the garlic, olive oil, and salt in a

small baking pan, such as a loaf pan, ramekin, or custard dish. Add only enough water to cover, and bake for about 1 hour, or until the cloves are brown in places and soft. Start checking occasionally after a half hour to make sure they don't burn.

2 Remove from the oven and let cool.

Sautéed Mushrooms

Raw mushrooms on a pizza are dry and tasteless. They never cook. Sautéing them first releases their flavor and makes them tender and juicy. I always wash my mushrooms. Despite what you may have heard about mushrooms soaking up water, you can't justify not washing something that grows in a pile of peat moss mixed with manure. The water they soak up is negligible, and any lingering water will help the mushrooms steam a little as they cook.

To save time: Sauté the mushrooms a few days in advance. They will last for 3 days if wrapped and stored in your refrigerator. Once reheated on the pizza, the mushrooms will be as fresh as when they first came out of the pan.

INGREDIENTS

¼ pound (100 g) large white mushrooms, pre-sliced white mushrooms, or button mushrooms (about 2 cups sliced)

1½ teaspoons extra virgin olive oil or Herbed Grill Oil (page 28)

¼ teaspoon salt

Pinch of freshly ground black pepper

Makes enough sautéed mushrooms for 1 pizza

1 Wash the mushrooms right before cooking. (If you wash them and put them back in the refrigerator, the next day they will darken and soften a little.) Rinse them well while rubbing them with your hands. Pat them dry with paper towels. Slice thinly if you are using whole mushrooms.

2 Heat the olive oil in a sauté pan on medium-high heat. Add the mushrooms and sauté until soft, about 3 minutes. Season with salt and pepper.

Building Your Own Pizza

A grilled crust or piadina is a blank canvas, waiting to become your masterpiece. It's all about finding a perfect mix of flavor, texture, and color. Here are the guidelines I use.

Taste

The secret is yin and yang, how opposites attract. Hot flavors such as jalapeño, habanero, or chili powder need a cool or sweet counterpart to bring complexity to the heat. Fruits excite the taste buds and create big flavor contrasts by cooling this heat. Try mango, peach, or apple.

Flavors that are spicy but not necessarily hot, such as cumin, curry powder, mustard, and ginger, find balance when paired with smooth, cool, or crisp flavors such as cucumber, avocado, or persimmon.

Salty proteins such as prosciutto, Parmesan, blue cheese, or anchovy are terrific when paired with sweet caramelized figs or dates, or grilled pineapple and cantaloupe.

Add a final bright note of flavor with a last minute garnish of fresh chopped herbs.

Texture

The same rule of opposites applies here. If you start with a purée or creamy cheese as a base, you need crispiness and crunch. Add toasted nuts, seeds, or raw vegetables. Or finish off a pizza with a crunchy sprinkle of bacon pieces.

Even a pizza as simple as the Margheritan (page 110) has hidden complexities. First there's a crisp and smoky thin crust. Then the silky Herbed Grill Oil coats the palate with its fruity, rich flavors. The salty, earthy tones of Parmesan cheese hit the back of the palate. A buttery layer of melted mozzarella comes next. When topped with my Chunky Tomato Basil Sauce, its tart yet sweet tones are then infused with basil's floral spiciness.

Try tasting a few different ingredients together first before putting them on a pizza to see if the textural components work for you.

Color and shapes

The variety of color and shapes is the first thing people notice, and it only increases their anticipation of pleasure. Grilled pizzas can be more colorful than traditional baked pizzas because the toppings are cooked for a short time, leaving more of their natural nutritional value and color.

Play the colors and shapes of ingredients off one another and keep each component distinct. Go for a mosaic pattern rather than a big pile. The Margheritan, for example, creates lots of eye appeal with its red tomato sauce, green basil leaves, and white pillows of fresh mozzarella, all within a brown and black-charred crust.

Putting It All Together

Now that you've got the theory down, here's how to create your own pizza or piadina. Take your cues from the previous page and build your own pizza, starting with flavor combinations, then alternating textures, and finishing with beautiful colors and shapes.

1 Brush the grilled side of the crust with 1 tablespoon of Herbed Grill Oil (page 28).

2 Add 1 tablespoon of grated Parmesan to deepen the flavor of milder cheese to come.

3 Follow with a ½ cup of shredded mozzarella or Fontina. Add or substitute more cheese as you wish. Choose cheeses that melt well, such as white Cheddar or Provolone. Melted cheese helps hold the toppings on the pizza.

4 Add a sauce. Add 1 cup of Chunky Tomato Basil Sauce or Basil Pecan Pesto. I like to drop spoonfuls of my sauce over the pizza instead of spreading it into an even coat. This creates a pretty pattern and results in different tastes in each bite.

5 Follow with toppings. Go for a variety of flavors, textures, and colors. See my suggested selections at right.

6 Add a garnish. Sprinkle chopped Italian parsley or cilantro, a few leaves of fresh basil, or pile some salad greens, lightly dressed, on top.

My parting advice: Less is more. Go for artistic taste combinations rather than the loaded approach. If the pizza is too heavy it will be difficult to maneuver on the grill and even harder to eat.

VEGETABLE TOPPINGS

- Roasted red pepper strips
- Red onions, thinly sliced
- Olives, thinly sliced or halved Capers
- Artichoke hearts, quartered
- Sautéed Mushrooms (page 32)
- Roasted Garlic Cloves (page 31)
- Spinach, quickly sautéed
- Jalapeños, thinly sliced

MEAT, POULTRY, OR SEAFOOD TOPPINGS

- Torn or rolled prosciutto or salami
- Crumbled bacon
- Sliced grilled sausage or pepperoni
- Grilled Chicken Breast, torn in chunks (page 29)
- Smoked salmon, torn or rolled
- Shrimp, quickly sautéed

CHEESE, NUT, OR FRUIT TOPPINGS

- Crumbled Gorgonzola or feta
- Toasted walnuts or pine nuts
- Sliced mango, pears, persimmon, or apples
- Grilled peaches or pineapple

Grilling a pizza or piadina on all kinds of cooking surfaces is easy. For outdoor grilling, you'll start with a medium-hot fire for the crust, and then move to indirect heat to grill the pizza. I like to broil the finished pizza in the oven for a minute or two afterward to crisp the toppings and heat the pizza through, but that's not essential. Next, I'll show you how to grill pizzas and piadinas indoors, on everything from skillets to clamshell grills, and even in your fireplace.

Grilling

Outdoor Grilling Methods

You're going to grill in two steps. First, grill the crust, on one side only. Turn it over and use the browned side to build the pizza before sliding it back on the grill. This method results in a crispy yet soft crust, and builds in more flavor because both sides of the crust are grilled. I use long-handled tongs to move the pizza around. Clean your grill before setting up (see page 13).

Charcoal grill

1 Remove the grate from the grill. Place a charcoal chimney inside and fill it with charcoal.

2 Stuff a crumpled sheet of newspaper in the lower compartment of the chimney. Or rip off the top of the charcoal bag. I like this method because as I use the charcoal, my bag gets smaller and smaller. When the charcoal is gone, so is the bag.

3 Light the crumpled paper through the holes in the bottom of the chimney. Long spark igniters or gas wands work well. A long match is fine too. The coals should be ready in 15 minutes.

4 Once the coals are covered in white ash, it is time to spread them out. Carefully lift the

IF YOU DON'T HAVE A CHIMNEY

Place a small pile of coals about the size of a football in the bottom of the grill, and start your coals with paraffin cakes, little patties made of wax and wood. Layering newspaper and charcoal works too, but it can take a long time to get going.

chimney by the handle and pour the coals out into the grill. (For a gas-starter charcoal grill, refer to the manufacturer's directions for starting the charcoal. It should take about 10 minutes to heat.)

5 Spread the coals in a single layer in the middle of the grill, using long tongs or a grill fork. Create a circle of coals as wide as the pizza. You should have a medium heat fire, all gray coals with ashes. Hold your hand 6 inches (15 cm) from the surface of the grill and count to six. If your hand does not get hot, your fire may be too cool. Open the side vents of the grill and let in more air so the coals burn faster and get hotter.

   On the other hand, if you have fiery red coals, the fire is too hot. Close the vents halfway to slow it down. The vents help control airflow, which in turn controls the fire's heat.

6 Place the grate back on the grill and let it heat for about 5 minutes before grilling. Wipe it quickly with a wad of paper towels to remove any soot.

Gas grill

Follow the manufacturer's directions to ignite the gas and light the burners. Adjust each burner to the medium-high setting. Close the grill cover and allow the grill to heat for about 10 minutes, or until the thermometer reaches 400°F (200°C).

Grilling the crust

1 When your grill is at the right temperature, hold the cookie sheet close to it and slide the dough onto the grill. If the dough folds in on itself, try to move the edges out quickly to form a flat crust (without burning yourself!). As long as the crust is about 12 x 12 inches (30 x 30 cm), don't worry if the shape is irregular. This is one of the best characteristics about grilled pizza: It is meant to look rustic and unrefined.

2 The dough should take about 3 minutes to cook. Watch for bubbles. The crust will be soft at first and tear easily, so try not to touch it. Soon it will set and firm up.

3 To check whether your crust is done, lift the underside. It should be an even light brown with brown grill marks. A charred crust adds to the flavor.

4 Pick up the crust from the middle, using tongs, and place it on your cookie sheet. Flip it over so the grilled side is face up. This browned side becomes the top of your pizza.

Variation: For thicker crust dough, use a slightly cooler fire and grill a few minutes longer. This way the outer crust does not burn before the middle of the dough cooks through.

Grilling the pizza

By now you have topped your crust and are ready to grill your pizza. I hope you used a spare approach, as a loaded pizza becomes difficult to maneuver on the grill. And a spare pizza results in a different taste in each bite, rather than a uniform bite of each ingredient.

1 The grill should still be medium-hot from grilling the crust. Now you will shift to indirect heat. If you have been away from the grill for a while and the fire has cooled, add enough coals to get back to the amount you started with, and wait a few minutes until the fire is hot again. (If you have a gas grill, turn the fire down to about 75 percent of the highest heat.)

2 Take off the grate and move the coals to one side of the grill. Replace the grate.

3 Bring your pizza, on its cookie sheet or pizza screen, next to the grill. Slide long tongs into the middle of the pizza and grip it firmly, then slide the pizza onto the grill, guiding it to the opposite side of the hot coals.

4 Preheat your oven's broiler, if desired. Grill your pizza for 5 to 8 minutes. Check it after 1 minute by gently lifting up an edge of the crust with your tongs or spatula. If it is turning dark quickly, your fire is too hot. Move the pizza around the grill to get away from the heat. Conversely, you can slide it directly over the fire for a brief moment to brown spots that don't seem done. I like to turn it twice during the grilling process to get an even doneness.

  After 3 to 4 minutes, the pizza will begin to crisp and brown lightly on the bottom. When it's done, the crust will be crispy. If the bottom has a few black spots, don't freak out. You have not burned it. Some charring is natural, and this is a delicious part of the crust.

4

Grip the pizza in the middle with your tongs
and pull it onto your cookie sheet.

5 Optional: For browned toppings or to thicken
   or caramelize glazes, some pizzas benefit
   from a quick broil in your oven. Broil the
   pizza, right on the cookie sheet, for 1 to 2
   minutes, or until the top is sizzling hot. Don't
   turn your back, or it may burn.

6 Slide the pizza onto a cutting board. Garnish
   as your recipe indicates. Cut it into squares or
   pie-shaped slices. Serve immediately.

WORK IN ADVANCE

If you don't want to grill both the crusts and the
pizzas when entertaining, grill the crusts ahead of
time. That way, when guests come over, you just
pull out your crusts, add the toppings, and slide
them onto the grill. Grilled crusts keep in your
refrigerator for up to 3 days, or in the freezer for up
to a month. Keep them tightly wrapped in plastic so
they will not dry out. To defrost frozen crusts, thaw
in the refrigerator for 2 hours, or on the counter at
room temperature for 20 to 30 minutes.

Indoor Grilling Methods

Grilling a crust indoors is simple and yields surprisingly good results. Just roll the dough out to a size the appliance can accomodate, and get the appliance as hot as possible. This requires preheating for at least 5 minutes. I tested every indoor grill I could find as I wanted the methods to be easy, but the result had to taste as good as outdoor pizza.

Cast-iron grill pan

Wipe the bottom of the pan with a paper towel moistened with olive oil. Preheat the pan over medium-high heat for 5 minutes. Sprinkle a cookie sheet with no sides with cornmeal.

1 Pick up the dough with both hands and lay it in the hot pan. The crust should bubble on top within 1 minute. If not, turn up the heat a little.

2 After 2 minutes, check the crust by lifting an edge with your tongs. When the bottom turns brown, remove it to the cookie sheet.

3 Turn the crust over and brush the crust with Herbed Grill Oil (page 28). Preheat your broiler.

4 Continue to add toppings as per your recipe.

5 Reheat your grilling pan for about 1 minute. Slide the pizza back into it and brown the bottom until crispy, 3 to 5 minutes. Turn it around a couple of times to ensure even browning.

6 Grasp the pizza and look at the underside. It should be golden and crisp with grill marks.

7 Place the pizza under the broiler and broil for about 1 minute until the top is sizzling hot.

Take care that it doesn't burn.

8 Transfer the pizza to a cutting board
   and add garnish as your recipe indicates.
   Cut into square or pie-shaped pieces
   and serve immediately.

Flat griddle

This works as well as the grill pan, without the lines. If the griddle is too small for a 12-inch (30 cm) pizza, tear off a piece of dough about the size of a golf ball, then roll out the remainder into an 8- to 10-inch (20 to 25 cm) pizza crust. Sprinkle a little cornmeal on a cookie sheet with no sides or on the flipside of a cookie sheet, and place the crust on the cornmeal.

1 Preheat the griddle on the highest setting for about 10 minutes. Preheat your oven broiler. Slide the dough onto the hot griddle and cook for about 5 minutes.

2 When it's ready, the crust will be bubbling and light brown on the bottom.

3 Remove the crust with tongs and place it back on the cookie sheet. Oil both sides with 1 tablespoon of Herbed Grill Oil or butter. Add the appropriate toppings to the grilled side, depending on your recipe.

4 Return the pizza to the hot griddle and cook for about 8 minutes, or until the bottom becomes crisp. Slide the pizza onto the cookie sheet and place it beneath the broiler for 1 to 2 minutes, until sizzling hot. Watch it so it doesn't burn.

5 Transfer to a cutting board and garnish as your recipe indicates. Cut into square or pie-shaped pieces and serve immediately.

Panini grill

This grill makes an amazingly crispy thin crust with perfect grill marks. Use these same instructions for a contact grill press.

1 Preheat your grill on high for about 10 minutes. Pick up the dough with both hands and gently lay it on the bottom grill. Close the grill and cook the crust for 2 to 3 minutes. Meanwhile, preheat your broiler oven.

2 Open it and peek. If the crust is browning, it is ready. If the crust looks a little pale, close the grill again and cook for 30 seconds to 1 minute longer. Do not overbrown the crust or it will be too crisp.

3 Open the grill and take out the crust, using tongs. Place it on the flipside of a cookie sheet. Oil the top with 1 tablespoon Herbed Grill Oil or butter, and add toppings as the recipe

4

indicates. To cook the topping, place the cookie sheet beneath the broiler for 1 to 2 minutes, until sizzling hot. Watch it so it doesn't burn.

4 Transfer to a cutting board and garnish as your recipe indicates. Cut into square or pie-shaped pieces and serve immediately.

TUSCAN OR FIREPLACE GRILL

Gathering in front of a fireplace to grill is a warm and cozy experience. The fireplace produces the smokiest flavor of all the grilling methods because the pizza cooks over seasoned wood. Also, the fireplace is like a natural smoker, with smoke rushing up through the grill and flavoring the pizza. Grilling in a fireplace seems tricky. But if you use a few tools to handle the situation, you will find it is quite rewarding.

1 Start with a good seasoned hardwood, such as hickory, oak, or alder. Never use a soft wood like pine because it creates too much residue and soot.

2 Build a large fire toward the back of the fireplace about 1 hour before grilling. Let the fire burn down to create plenty of embers. Place your grill in front of the burning logs. Gather a bed of embers at least 1 inch deep under the whole grill area, using your fireplace shovel. Try for an even bed.

3 Add some logs to the fire in the back to keep it burning. Your grill should be hot enough in about 5 minutes. You will know it is ready by holding your hand about 6 inches (15 cm) over the grill and counting slowly. If you cannot reach number 6 before you have to take your hand away, it's ready. If not, add more embers from the logs.

4 Now you are ready to grill your crust and pizza as you would on an outdoor grill. See directions on page 38.

Pizzas
with Meat

The Chicagoan
Grilled steak, baked potato, and sour cream

I am a Chicago guy, born and raised in the Windy City. I left to travel the world and learn about cooking, but Chicago called me back home. Chicagoans love meat, and the city has always been a leader in producing the nation's best beef. Steaks really are bigger in our restaurants. So are the baked potatoes that appear alongside them, topped with sour cream and chives. They taste fantastic on a grilled pizza.

To save time: Roast the sliced potatoes ahead of time but do not refrigerate them, or you'll lose some flavor and texture.

1 Preheat the oven to 400°F (200°C). Place the sliced potato in a large bowl and toss with the olive oil, salt, and pepper. Line a baking sheet with foil and spread the slices in a single layer. Bake for about 15 minutes, until the potato is golden and tender. While still hot, loosen the slices with a spatula so they don't stick.

2 Prepare a grill for direct cooking over high heat. Season the steak liberally on both sides with the salt and pepper. Grill the steak over the hottest part of the fire for 4 minutes. Turn and grill for 4 minutes longer, until the steak is medium-rare and well charred. Remove and let sit for 5 minutes. Slice thinly.

3 Brush the grilled side of the pizza crust with the Herbed Grill Oil and dust with the Parmesan. Sprinkle the mozzarella and Cheddar on top. Drop spoonfuls of the Chunky Tomato Basil Sauce onto the pizza. Top with the potato, red onion, and steak.

4 Grill the pizza according to Chapter 4. Before serving, drop teaspoons of the sour cream onto the pizza, and garnish with the fresh chives.

INGREDIENTS

Roasted Potatoes

1 Russet potato, peeled and sliced about ¼ inch (6 mm) thick

2 tablespoons extra virgin olive oil

1 teaspoon salt

½ teaspoon freshly ground black pepper

8 ounces (225 g) top sirloin or strip steak

½ teaspoon salt

Freshly ground black pepper

1 grilled pizza crust

1 tablespoon Herbed Grill Oil (page 28) or extra virgin olive oil

1 tablespoon grated Parmesan

1 cup shredded mozzarella

½ cup shredded Cheddar

1 cup Chunky Tomato Basil Sauce (page 28)

½ cup thinly sliced red onions

Garnish

¼ cup sour cream

2 tablespoons minced fresh chives

The Emilian
Prosciutto with caramelized cantaloupe chutney

Parma, a city in the Italian region of Emilia-Romagna, gives its name to two famous foods produced there: Prosciutto di Parma and Parmesan cheese. Prosciutto is Italian ham that takes anywhere from 9 to 24 months to dry cure. Only experts who know the right conditions for the meat can process it. Back in the 1800s, the Duchess of Parma, Napoleon's second wife, found the combination of prosciutto and melon delightful. I've incorporated this taste as well as other flavors to further enhance the irresistible sweet and salty combination. Freeze the Fontina cheese for a half hour before using to make it easier to shred.

To save time: Make the Cantaloupe Chutney up to 3 days in advance.

1 To make the Cantaloupe Chutney, put the sugar and water in a small skillet over medium heat. Stir constantly until it turns a light golden brown, about 8 minutes. If the sugar hardens into lumps, don't worry, it will melt as the chutney cooks.

2 Add the cantaloupe, jalapeño, and vinegar and stir. Reduce the heat to medium low. Cook until most of the liquid is gone and the chutney is thick, about 10 minutes. Stir occasionally so it doesn't burn on the bottom. Remove from the heat and stir in the olive oil.

3 Brush the grilled side of the pizza crust with the Herbed Grill Oil. Sprinkle on the Parmesan, mozzarella, and Fontina. Drop spoonfuls of the Cantaloupe Chutney on top, then add the prosciutto in bunched-up slices, filling in the spots to make a colorful pattern. Sprinkle the Gorgonzola over all.

4 Grill the pizza according to Chapter 4. When the pizza is ready to be served, sprinkle on the chopped walnuts and sage, if desired.

INGREDIENTS

Cantaloupe Chutney

¼ cup sugar

1 tablespoon water

1 cup ripe cantaloupe, chopped into ½-inch cubes

½ fresh jalapeño, seeded and minced (see Note)

1 tablespoon red wine vinegar

1 teaspoon extra virgin olive oil

1 grilled pizza crust

1 tablespoon Herbed Grill Oil (page 28) or extra virgin olive oil

1 tablespoon grated Parmesan

½ cup shredded mozzarella

½ cup grated Fontina

3 ounces (75 g) prosciutto, about 9 slices

¾ cup crumbled Gorgonzola

Garnish

2 tablespoons roasted walnuts, chopped

4 fresh sage leaves, whole or chopped (optional)

Note: When working with hot peppers such as jalapeños, do not touch your eyes. Wash your hands, utensils, and cutting board thoroughly as soon as you are finished.

The Jamaican
Jerk-smoked pork with plum chutney and mango

The first time I tasted prune juice, I was surprised that I enjoyed it and right away I wanted to work it into a pizza. That's how the Jamaican was born. This combination of sweet, sour, spicy, hot, and smoky was good enough to win first place in its category at the Las Vegas International Pizza Competition in 2000. Buy the mango a few days in advance to let it ripen. Choose one with taut skin and no soft spots.

To save time: Prepare the Dark Plum Chutney up to 3 days in advance.

1 To make the Dark Plum Chutney, mix all the ingredients together in a small saucepan. Bring to a boil and simmer over low heat for about 10 minutes. The sauce should be slightly thick, spicy, and sweet.

2 Rub the pork with Liquid Smoke, followed by the dry rub. Grill over medium hot coals, or sauté in a skillet over medium heat, until cooked through, about 20 minutes. When the pork is ready, it will be tender and easily torn apart. Let the meat cool slightly, and tear it into chunks, discarding any bits of cartilage, fat, or gristle.

3 Brush the grilled side of the pizza crust with the Herbed Grill Oil. Dust with the Parmesan and then with the mozzarella. Drop spoonfuls of the Chunky Tomato Basil Sauce onto the pizza.

4 Add the pork pieces, followed by the mango, in an alternating pattern. Drizzle the Dark Plum Chutney over all.

5 Grill the pizza according to Chapter 4. Garnish with the cilantro before serving.

INGREDIENTS

Dark Plum Chutney

½ cup prune juice

2 tablespoons brown sugar

½ teaspoon dried ground ginger

¼ cup dark raisins

1 teaspoon cornstarch

¼ teaspoon chili flakes

Smoked Pork

One 8-ounce (225 g) boneless pork steak, from shoulder blade or butt; or boneless ribs

1 teaspoon Liquid Smoke

1 tablespoon jerk-spice dry rub

1 grilled pizza crust

1 tablespoon Herbed Grill Oil (page 28) or extra virgin olive oil

1 tablespoon grated Parmesan

1 cup shredded mozzarella

½ cup Chunky Tomato Basil Sauce (page 28)

½ ripe mango, cut into ¼-inch (6 mm) slices

Garnish

2 tablespoons cilantro leaves

The Millennium
Ground lamb, feta, and Kalamata olives

Remember the Y2K thing that had everyone in a tizzy about 2000? People were stocking arms, water, food, batteries— everything they thought they would need when the lights went out and the savages started looting and pillaging. At the time, I did my own preparations: I made a grilled pizza! Since a millennium is a thousand years, I turned to ancient Greece for inspiration. I combined ground lamb, feta cheese, and Kalamata olives to create this mouthwatering grilled pizza. Don't wait a thousand years to make it.

1 To make the Spiced Lamb, brown the meat over high heat in a medium skillet. Add the remaining ingredients and simmer for 5 minutes.

2 Brush the grilled side of the pizza crust with the Herbed Grill Oil. Dust with the Parmesan and sprinkle with the mozzarella. Drop spoonfuls of the Chunky Tomato Basil Sauce on top. Add the onions, garlic, olives, feta, and Spiced Lamb.

3 Grill the pizza according to Chapter 4. Before serving, garnish the pizza with the cucumber and oregano.

INGREDIENTS

Spiced Lamb

8 ounces (225 g) ground lamb or ground beef

1 teaspoon dried oregano

½ teaspoon dried thyme

¼ teaspoon ground allspice

½ teaspoon salt

½ teaspoon freshly ground black pepper

1 clove garlic, minced

2 tablespoons red wine vinegar

1 grilled pizza crust

1 tablespoon Herbed Grill Oil (page 28) or extra virgin olive oil

1 tablespoon grated Parmesan

1 cup shredded mozzarella

1 cup Chunky Tomato Basil Sauce (page 28)

½ cup thinly sliced red onions

2 cloves garlic, thinly sliced

12 pitted Kalamata olives, halved

½ cup crumbled feta

Garnish

½ cup peeled and diced cucumber

2 tablespoons fresh oregano leaves

The Olympian

Sausage, pepperoni, artichoke hearts, and peppers

In 1996, the summer Olympics came to Atlanta. The first event was a cross-country relay that ended when the runner lit the Olympic flame at the opening ceremony. Karla and I found out he would pass right in front of our pizzeria, and we decided to capitalize on the crowd. We rented a helium tank and filled the restaurant with hundreds of balloons to make it more festive. When we opened the restaurant, we were slammed immediately by two dozen kindergarteners and their mommies. The kids ran around our restaurant, took our free balloons, asked for water, and used our bathroom. We took it on the chin that day. But we did see the torch runner pass by. In honor of the Olympics, I created a pizza that contains one ingredient from six countries. Its satisfying combination of saltiness and crunch makes it a crowd pleaser.

1   Brush the grilled side of the pizza crust with the Herbed Grill Oil. Dust with the Parmesan and sprinkle with the mozzarella, then drop spoonfuls of the Chunky Tomato Basil Sauce on top. Add the sausage, pepperoni, artichoke hearts, sun-dried tomatoes, feta, green peppers, and olives.

2   Grill the pizza according to Chapter 4. Before serving, garnish it with the parsley, if desired.

INGREDIENTS

1 grilled pizza crust

1 tablespoon Herbed Grill Oil (page 28) or extra virgin olive oil

1 tablespoon grated Parmesan

1 cup shredded mozzarella

1 cup Chunky Tomato Basil Sauce (page 28)

4 ounces (100 g) smoked sausage, sliced into coins (Poland)

1 ounce (25 g) pepperoni, about 16 slices (Italy)

5 artichoke hearts, quartered, about half a 13¾-ounce (375 g) can (Belgium)

2 halves sun-dried tomatoes, sliced into ribbons (Italy)

½ cup crumbled feta (Greece)

¼ cup diced green peppers (United States)

2 tablespoons sliced black olives, about 6 (Spain)

Garnish (optional)

1 tablespoon fresh Italian parsley, chopped

Parma e Fiche
Prosciutto, figs, and Gorgonzola

People always say, "Wow, this is serious," when I make this pizza. The combination of syrupy figs, salty prosciutto, and rich Gorgonzola makes this pizza satisfying and decadent. If it's not the season for fresh figs, soak dried figs in water overnight, and use the leftover soaking water instead of the apple juice. Freeze the Fontina for a half hour before use to make it easier to shred.

To save time: Make the figs up to 3 days ahead.

1 Remove the fig stems and cut the figs in half. Place the figs, apple juice, and brown sugar in a wide skillet and cook on medium heat until the sauce becomes syrupy, about 15 minutes. Stir occasionally to make sure the syrup doesn't burn. (For fresh figs, be gentle to keep them from breaking down.) Remove from the heat and stir in the butter. Cool slightly.

2 Brush the grilled side of the pizza crust with the Herbed Grill Oil. Next, sprinkle on the Parmesan and top with the mozzarella and Fontina. Drop spoonfuls of the figs and their syrup over the pizza. Place the prosciutto slices on the pizza in bunches, creating an alternating pattern. Top with the crumbled Gorgonzola.

3 Grill the pizza according to Chapter 4. Garnish with the chopped parsley, if desired, before serving.

INGREDIENTS

12 fresh figs (about 8 ounces/225 g) or 8 dried figs (about 6 ounces/175 g)

½ cup apple juice

½ cup brown sugar

1 tablespoon unsalted butter

1 grilled pizza crust

1 tablespoon Herbed Grill Oil (page 28) or extra virgin olive oil

1 tablespoon grated Parmesan

½ cup shredded mozzarella

½ cup shredded Fontina

3 ounces/75 g prosciutto, about 9 slices

½ cup crumbled Gorgonzola or blue cheese

Garnish (optional)

1 tablespoon chopped fresh Italian parsley

The Santa Fe
Spicy ground beef, cheese, and crisp lettuce

Santa Fe's Southwestern food is one of the best regional cuisines anywhere. I love the bright flavors of chiles, tomatoes, and garlic, and the spicy meat that fills everything from peppers to squash blossoms to tortillas. This pizza has Santa Fe's flair, with its bold cheesy and spicy meat beneath crisp lettuce. I've made this pizza for New Mexicans, who enjoy the homage this grilled pizza pays to their cuisine.

1 Heat a large skillet over medium heat. Crumble the ground beef into the skillet and stir in half the taco spice mix. Cook until the meat is thoroughly browned, and drain if needed.

2 Brush the grilled side of the pizza crust with the Herbed Grill Oil. Dust with the Parmesan and the remaining taco spice mix. Sprinkle the mozzarella and Longhorn Colby over the crust, then drop spoonfuls of the Chunky Tomato Basil Sauce on top. Finally, sprinkle the cooked ground beef over all.

3 Grill the pizza according to Chapter 4. Just before serving, top the pizza with the shredded lettuce and sprinkle with the tomato, red onions, olives, jalapeño, and cilantro. Dot with teaspoons of the sour cream.

INGREDIENTS

8 ounces (225 g) ground beef

1 packet taco spice mix, preferably McCormick's or El Paso's

1 grilled pizza crust

1 tablespoon Herbed Grill Oil (page 28) or extra virgin olive oil

1 tablespoon grated Parmesan

½ cup shredded Mozzarella

½ cup shredded Longhorn Colby

1 cup Chunky Tomato Basil Sauce (page 28)

Garnish

1 cup shredded iceberg or Romaine lettuce

1 small tomato, diced (about ¼ cup)

½ cup thinly sliced red onions

2 tablespoons sliced black olives

1 jalapeño pepper, seeded and sliced (see Note)

1 tablespoon cilantro, chopped

3 tablespoons sour cream

Note: When working with hot peppers such as jalapeños, do not touch your eyes. Wash your hands, utensils, and cutting board thoroughly as soon as you are finished.

The Pennsylvanian

Smoked sausage with honey mustard and coleslaw

Many of America's early German immigrants settled in Pennsylvania. Germans are called *Deutsch* in their own language, and eventually they came to be called "Pennsylvania Dutch." These folks use sweet and sour flavors to accent their irresistible smoked sausages, hams, and bacon. I couldn't wait to try it. For this pizza, I start with a smoked sausage and cheese pizza, drizzle it with a honey mustard, and cover it with tangy coleslaw to represent all aspects of Pennsylvania Dutch cuisine.

To save time: Buy coleslaw mix (shredded cabbage and carrots) from the produce department of your supermarket. Prepare the coleslaw up to 2 hours in advance. Prepare the Honey Mustard Glaze in advance and refrigerate it for up to 1 month.

1 To make the Sweet and Sour Coleslaw, place the olive oil, vinegar, and sugar in a medium bowl. Season with the salt and pepper and mix well. Add the cabbage and carrots and mix well. Chill for one hour to let the flavors blend.

2 For the Honey Mustard Glaze, place all of the ingredients in a small bowl. Season with salt and pepper and mix well.

3 Prepare a hot grill. Char the smoked sausage until brown, about 7 minutes. Cut the sausage into small chunks.

4 Brush the grilled side of the pizza crust with the Herbed Grill Oil. Dust with the Parmesan and sprinkle with the mozzarella and Cheddar. Top with the sausage chunks and the red onions. Drizzle the Honey Mustard Glaze over all.

5 Grill the pizza according to Chapter 4. Just before serving, place spoonfuls of the Sweet and Sour Coleslaw on top.

INGREDIENTS

Sweet and Sour Coleslaw

1 tablespoon extra virgin olive oil

1 teaspoon vinegar

1 teaspoon sugar

Kosher salt and freshly ground black pepper

1 cup shredded green or red cabbage

¼ cup peeled, shredded carrots

Honey Mustard Glaze

½ cup Dijon mustard

¼ cup honey

Pinch of red pepper flakes

Kosher salt and freshly ground black pepper

8 ounces (225 g) smoked sausage, preferably knockwurst or kielbasa

1 grilled pizza crust

1 tablespoon Herbed Grill Oil (page 28) or extra virgin olive oil

1 tablespoon Parmesan

½ cup shredded mozzarella

½ cup shredded Cheddar

½ cup diced red onions

The Trattorian

Sausage, pepperoni, mushrooms, and bacon

One of the first pizzas on my restaurant menu was the Trattorian. I named it for trattorias in Italy that serve traditional Italian food, because the Trattorian is a traditional pizza. In 2001, I entered the Mid-American Pizza Competition, which showcases the best pizzas from mid-America and pits them against one another. The Trattorian won second place in the traditional pizza category.

1 Brush the grilled side of the pizza crust with the Herbed Grill Oil. Dust the crust with the Parmesan and sprinkle the mozzarella over it. Drop spoonfuls of the Chunky Tomato Basil Sauce on top. Add the pepperoni, sausage, mushrooms, red onions, bacon, and green peppers, in an alternating pattern.

2 Grill the pizza according to Chapter 4.

INGREDIENTS

1 grilled pizza crust

1 tablespoon Herbed Grill Oil (page 28) or extra virgin olive oil

1 tablespoon grated Parmesan

1 cup shredded mozzarella

1 cup Chunky Tomato Basil Sauce (page 28)

1 ounce (25 g) pepperoni, about 16 slices

1 hot Italian sausage link, about 8 inches (20 cm), cooked and sliced thin

½ recipe Sautéed Mushrooms (page 32)

½ cup thinly sliced red onions

4 strips hickory-smoked bacon, cooked crisp and crumbled

½ cup thinly sliced green peppers

The Venetian

Soppressata, onion marmalade, and walnuts

In Venetian cuisine there's a savory marmalade called *saor*, made of golden brown onions and cooked with vinegar and a little sugar. Traditionally, it is served with fish, pine nuts, and raisins, but I prefer it paired with another Italian delicacy called soppressata, a type of dry salami. It comes in two varieties, hot and sweet. I prefer the hot for its spiciness, but the sweet one is good too. Imported or artisan soppressata is best. You'll notice a big difference in flavor compared to domestic. If you can't find soppressata at all, substitute Genoa salami.

1 Heat the olive oil in a deep skillet on medium heat. Add the onions and sugar. Cook the onions, stirring frequently, until they turn light brown, about 25 minutes. Reduce the heat to low. Let it cool for a minute, and then add the balsamic vinegar and salt. Cook until the vinegar is absorbed, about 2 minutes. Remove from the heat and let cool.

2 Brush the grilled side of the pizza crust with the Herbed Grill Oil. Dust the crust with the Parmesan and sprinkle the mozzarella on top. Drop spoonfuls of the Onion Marmalade on the pizza, alternating with bunched-up slices of soppressata. Do not lay the slices flat. Finally, top with the walnuts.

3 Grill the pizza according to Chapter 4. Garnish with the fresh parsley, if desired, before serving.

INGREDIENTS

Onion Marmalade

3 tablespoons extra virgin olive oil

2 medium yellow onions, thinly sliced

2 tablespoons sugar

2 tablespoons balsamic vinegar

½ teaspoon salt

1 grilled pizza crust

1 tablespoon Herbed Grill Oil (page 28) or extra virgin olive oil

1 tablespoon grated Parmesan

1 cup shredded mozzarella

2 ounces (50 g) thinly sliced soppressata, about 9 slices

¼ cup walnut halves

Garnish (optional)

1 tablespoon chopped fresh Italian parsley

Back in 1985, California Pizza Kitchen debuted a barbecued chicken pizza in its Beverly Hills restaurant. Today it's still the most popular pizza on the menu. While it's terrific and I've included a version in this chapter, there's lots more you can do with a chicken breast. Try drizzling it with brandied cherries, a honeyed curry sauce, Ranch dressing, or coconut sauce for starters. Your guests will be dazzled by your creativity.

Pizzas with Chicken

The Buffalo Wing

Spicy chicken with blue cheese and celery

Back in 1964, chicken wings cost five cents a pound and people used them for chicken soup. That changed in Buffalo, New York, when the owner of the Anchor Bar dumped a load of chicken wings into the fryer, tossed them in a spicy hot sauce, and served them with blue cheese dressing and celery sticks. Buffalo wings took off across the country. I love that flavor combination, so naturally, I created a buffalo-wing pizza. Because no one wants bones on a pizza, I use boneless chicken breast instead of wings, sautéed instead of deep-fried. This recipe calls for a cayenne and vinegar hot sauce, such as Frank's Red Hot Cayenne Pepper Sauce or Trappey's Red Devil Cayenne Pepper Sauce. Do not use Tabasco as a substitute. It is much hotter.

1 Slice the chicken breast into strips and season with salt and pepper. Heat the olive oil in a medium skillet on medium heat. Sauté the chicken strips for about 3 minutes until cooked through. Add the pepper sauce and stir for 1 minute, or until the sauce thickens slightly and clings to the chicken.

2 Heat 1 teaspoon of the Herbed Grill Oil in another medium skillet on medium heat. Add the celery, red onions, and red bell peppers. Sauté for 2 to 3 minutes until the vegetables become slightly limp.

3 Brush the grilled side of the pizza crust with the remaining 1 tablespoon of Herbed Grill Oil and dust with the Parmesan. Sprinkle the mozzarella and Cheddar on top. Drop spoonfuls of the Chunky Tomato Basil Sauce onto the pizza. Add the sautéed celery, red onions, and red bell peppers. Place the chicken strips on top, and finally, sprinkle with the crumbled blue cheese.

4 Grill the pizza according to Chapter 4. Garnish with the celery before serving.

INGREDIENTS

One 6-ounce (175 g) boneless, skinless chicken breast

Kosher salt and freshly ground black pepper

2 tablespoons extra virgin olive oil

½ cup cayenne pepper sauce

1 teaspoon, plus 1 tablespoon Herbed Grill Oil (page 28) or extra virgin olive oil

1 cup thinly sliced celery

½ cup thinly sliced red onions

½ cup thinly sliced red bell peppers

1 grilled pizza crust

1 tablespoon grated Parmesan

½ cup shredded mozzarella

½ cup shredded sharp Cheddar

½ cup Chunky Tomato Basil Sauce (page 28)

½ cup crumbled blue cheese

Garnish

¼ cup diced celery

The Cherry Bomb
Brandied cherry sauce and chicken

I first introduced this pizza at a fancy summer party for local celebrities that I catered in Chicago (the party and the pizza was covered in *Chicago* magazine). Since the party happened to be during the short cherry season, I wanted to feature the fruit. So this is my take on a classic entrée of roast chicken with cherry sauce. If cherries are not in season, use one 12- to 15-ounce (350–425 g) can of Bing cherries, drained and chopped.

1 Place the lime juice, orange juice, balsamic vinegar, salt, and cornstarch in a small bowl and stir well to combine.

2 Melt the butter in a small saucepan on medium heat. Add the lime zest and cherry preserves and stir for a minute or so, until the preserves melt. Add the cherries and brandy and stir to coat.

3 Pour the juice mix into the skillet, stir, and bring to a boil. Reduce the heat and simmer for 2 minutes, until the cherries are glazed and a little thick. Put the sauce in a small bowl and let cool a little.

4 Brush the grilled side of the pizza crust with the Herbed Grill Oil. Dust with the Parmesan. Sprinkle the mozzarella and Cheddar on top, followed by the chicken. Toss the cherries and sauce over all.

5 Grill the pizza on the grill according to Chapter 4. Garnish with the sage leaves, if desired, before serving.

INGREDIENTS

Cherry Sauce

2 tablespoons lime juice

2 tablespoons orange juice

1 tablespoon balsamic vinegar

¼ teaspoon salt

1 teaspoon cornstarch

1 tablespoon unsalted butter

Zest of 1 lime

1 tablespoon cherry or apricot preserves

½ pound (225 g) fresh Bing cherries, pits removed and sliced

1 tablespoon good brandy (plus more for sipping)

1 grilled pizza crust

1 tablespoon Herbed Grill Oil (page 28) or extra virgin olive oil

1 tablespoon Parmesan

½ cup shredded mozzarella

½ cup shredded sharp Cheddar

One 6-ounce (175 g) Grilled Chicken Breast (page 29), torn into bite-sized chunks

Garnish (optional)

Whole or chopped fresh sage leaves

The Moroccan

Curried chicken, roasted garlic, and Kalamata olives

In Morocco, people use flatbreads called *khubz* to eat spicy meats sold in the local marketplace. Merchants often baste these meats and poultry with curry powder and honey while grilling them. This sweet and spicy pizza is reminiscent of that Moroccan tradition, with its slightly charred crust and the grilled chicken glazed in curry spices and honey. It makes an excellent addition to any pizza party, and it will be the one people talk about long after the party is over.

1 Combine the Curry Glaze ingredients in a small bowl.

2 Brush the grilled side of the pizza crust with the Herbed Grill Oil. Dust the crust with the Parmesan, then sprinkle with the mozzarella. Add the chicken, red onions, roasted garlic, olives, and red peppers in an alternating pattern.

3 Drizzle the Curry Glaze over the entire pizza.

4 Grill the pizza according to Chapter 4, then broil it in the oven for up to 2 minutes to caramelize the glaze. Watch it closely to avoid burning. Garnish with the parsley, if desired, before serving.

INGREDIENTS

Curry Glaze

¼ cup honey

2 teaspoons curry powder

Pinch of red pepper flakes

Pinch of salt

1 grilled pizza crust

1 tablespoon Herbed Grill Oil (page 28) or extra virgin olive oil

1 tablespoon grated Parmesan

1 cup shredded mozzarella

One 6-ounce (175 g) Grilled Chicken Breast (page 29), torn into bite-sized chunks

½ cup thinly sliced red onions

12 Roasted Garlic Cloves (page 31)

12 pitted Kalamata olives, halved

¼ cup thinly sliced red peppers

Garnish (optional)

1 tablespoon Italian parsley leaves

The Ranch
Grilled Chicken with Ranch Dressing

Americans love their Ranch dressing. Even Homer Simpson can't get enough. In one episode of *The Simpsons*, he became bored with a harem of beautiful dancing women and asked for his Ranch dressing hose. The women appeared with a fire hose and blasted him with a geyser of it. They should have brought him this pizza. In it, I combine the dressing with chicken, bacon, and red onions. How can you go wrong?

1 Brush the grilled side of the pizza crust with the Herbed Grill Oil and dust with the Parmesan. Drop spoonfuls of the Ranch dressing onto the pizza without spreading it. Add an even layer of the mozzarella and Cheddar. Finally, top the pizza with the chicken, bacon, red onions, and tomato.

2 Grill the pizza according to Chapter 4. Garnish with the chives, if desired, before serving.

INGREDIENTS

1 grilled pizza crust

1 tablespoon Herbed Grill Oil (page 28)

1 tablespoon grated Parmesan

1/3 cup of your favorite Ranch dressing

1/2 cup shredded mozzarella

1/2 cup shredded sharp Cheddar

One 6-ounce (175 g) Grilled Chicken Breast (page 29), torn into bite-sized chunks

4 strips bacon, cooked crisp and crumbled

1/2 cup thinly sliced red onions

1 small tomato, diced (about 1/4 cup)

Garnish (optional)

1 tablespoon chopped fresh chives

The Texan
Barbecued chicken, cilantro, and cheese

This pizza is a cinch to make. I like to toss the chicken in barbecue sauce rather than spreading the sauce on the pizza. This technique still makes the pizza spicy and vinegary, but not too wet. If you want extra sauce, serve it on the side for dipping your pizza.

1   Place the chicken in a bowl. Add the barbecue sauce and toss to coat well.

2   Brush the grilled side of the pizza crust with the Herbed Grill Oil and dust with the Parmesan. Top with the mozzarella, then drop spoonfuls of the Chunky Tomato Basil sauce on top. Add the chicken, Cheddar, and red onions.

3   Grill the pizza according to Chapter 4. Top the finished pizza with the cilantro and the parsley, if desired. Serve with extra barbecue sauce on the side.

INGREDIENTS

One 6- to 8-ounce (175 to 225 g) Grilled Chicken Breast (page 29), torn into bite-sized chunks

4 tablespoons barbecue sauce, plus more for dipping

1 grilled pizza crust

1 tablespoon Herbed Grill Oil (page 28) or extra virgin olive oil

1 tablespoon grated Parmesan

½ cup shredded mozzarella

1 cup Chunky Tomato Basil Sauce (page 28)

½ cup shredded Cheddar

½ cup thinly sliced red onions

Garnish

1 tablespoon cilantro leaves

1 tablespoon chopped fresh Italian parsley (optional)

The Thai Pong Gari

Curried chicken with peanut sauce and salad

This pizza is inspired by chicken satay, with the flavors of curried chicken and peanut sauce. The refreshing salad on top adds crunch and juiciness. *Pong Gari* is the Thai name for the dry curry powder that finds its way into many Thai dishes. Peanut sauce is really a Western adaptation of Thai satay dipping sauce, which uses ground peanuts. I prefer the rich flavor of Japanese soy sauce, such as Kikkoman, rather than Chinese soy. While both are made from fermented soybeans, Chinese soy sauce is sometimes thickened with molasses.

1   Combine all of the Curry Glaze ingredients in a small bowl. In another small bowl, combine all of the Peanut Sauce ingredients.

2   Brush the grilled side of the pizza crust with the Herbed Grill Oil. Dust with the Parmesan and sprinkle the mozzarella on top. Next, drop spoonfuls of the Chunky Tomato Basil Sauce onto the pizza. Add the chicken and drizzle the Curry Glaze over all.

3   Grill the pizza according to Chapter 4. Just before serving, top the pizza with the salad ingredients. Drizzle the Thai Peanut Sauce over the salad.

INGREDIENTS

Curry Glaze

¼ cup honey

2 teaspoons curry powder

Pinch of red pepper flakes

Pinch of salt

Peanut Sauce

4 tablespoons smooth peanut butter

½ teaspoon minced fresh ginger

¼ teaspoon chili paste

2 tablespoons soy sauce

4 tablespoons water

1 grilled pizza crust

1 tablespoon Herbed Grill Oil (page 28) or extra virgin olive oil

1 tablespoon grated Parmesan

1 cup shredded mozzarella

½ cup Chunky Tomato Basil Sauce (page 28)

One 6-ounce (175 g) Grilled Chicken Breast (page 29), torn into bite-sized chunks

Salad

½ cup thinly sliced red peppers

1 cup bean sprouts

1 tablespoon sliced scallions

1 tablespoon coarsely chopped roasted peanuts

1 tablespoon coarsely chopped cilantro

The Venezuelan
Chicken and plantain with coconut sauce

Venezuelan cuisine is sweet, spicy, and earthy. Here, rich coconut and spicy coriander are matched by fresh chiles and mellowed by the fruity earthiness of plantain. I chose to use chicken because I thought it might go over better than goat, Venezuela's most popular meat. If you can't find a plantain, use a large green banana instead. Canned coconut milk brings island cuisine to you in a jiffy. Look for it in the ethnic or Asian aisle of your grocery store.

To save time: Make the Coconut Sauce up to 3 days in advance.

1 To make the Coconut Sauce, heat the sesame oil over medium heat in a large skillet. Add the onions, lime zest, and coriander and stir for about 1 minute. Add the lime juice, coconut milk, powdered sugar, and salt. Stir until combined well. Bring the sauce to a boil and simmer on medium heat until it becomes syrupy, about 5 minutes.

2 Combine the cayenne pepper and sugar in a large bowl. Add the plantain and toss to coat. Heat a medium skillet over medium heat and melt the butter. Add the seasoned plantain and sauté for about 5 minutes, stirring often until brown. Sprinkle with the salt while the plantain is still hot and moist.

3 Brush the grilled side of the pizza crust with Herbed Grill Oil. Dust with the Parmesan, followed by the Swiss or Fontina. Add the chicken and plantain in an alternating pattern. Drop spoonfuls of the Coconut Sauce onto the pizza. Sprinkle with the coconut.

4 Grill according to Chapter 4, then broil it in the oven for up to 2 minutes to toast the coconut. Watch it closely to avoid burning. Before serving, garnish with the jalapeño and cilantro.

INGREDIENTS

Coconut Sauce

1 teaspoon sesame oil

¼ cup diced onions

1 teaspoon lime zest

½ teaspoon ground coriander

1 tablespoon lime juice

1 cup coconut milk

2 tablespoons powdered sugar, packed

¼ teaspoon salt

½ teaspoon ground cayenne pepper

2 tablespoons sugar

1 small ripe plantain, peeled and diced into 1-inch (2½ cm) cubes

2 tablespoons unsalted butter

¼ teaspoon kosher salt

1 grilled pizza crust

1 tablespoon Herbed Grill Oil (page 28) or extra virgin olive oil

1 tablespoon Parmesan

1 cup shredded Swiss cheese or Fontina

One 6-ounce (175 g) Grilled Chicken Breast (page 29), torn into bite-sized chunks

¼ cup shaved or shredded coconut

Garnish

1 jalapeño chile pepper, minced

2 tablespoons cilantro leaves

The Vesuvian
Italian chicken with potatoes, Asiago, and olives

My Italian grandmother makes two great chicken dishes: Chicken Cacciatore and Chicken Vesuvio. The latter is an Old World dish from the Naples region of Italy, home of the famous Mount Vesuvius volcano. She douses chicken pieces in seasoned flour, and browns them in olive oil with white wine, onions, garlic, and potatoes until the flavors meld. I put some of the flavors of her Chicken Vesuvio on this grilled pizza to honor my grandmother, who is now ninety-three.

1 Place the chicken in a medium bowl and add the Italian dressing. Coat the chicken with the dressing and marinate for at least 1 hour, preferably overnight.

2 Prepare a medium-hot fire. Grill the chicken breast over the hottest part of a fire for about 10 minutes, depending on the thickness of the breast. Turn it once or twice. The meat is done when the juice runs clear when pierced with a knife tip. Do not overcook or the breast will dry out.

3 Preheat the oven to 400°F (200°C). Place the potato rounds on an oiled or sprayed baking sheet. Drizzle with 1 tablespoon of the Herbed Grill Oil and season with salt and pepper. Bake for about 20 minutes until browned.

4 Brush the grilled side of the pizza crust with the remaining tablespoon of Herbed Grill Oil and dust with the Parmesan. Sprinkle with the mozzarella and then top with the red onions, tomato, black olives, and Asiago. Add the potato rounds and chicken in an alternating pattern. Drizzle the remaining 2 tablespoons of Italian dressing over all.

5 Grill the pizza according to Chapter 4. Garnish with the parsley leaves, if desired, before serving.

INGREDIENTS

One 6-ounce (175 g) boneless, skinless chicken breast

1 cup of your favorite Italian dressing, plus 2 tablespoons for drizzling

4 small potatoes, sliced into ¼-inch (6 cm) rounds

Vegetable oil

2 tablespoons Herbed Grill Oil (page 28) or extra virgin olive oil

Salt and freshly ground black pepper

1 grilled pizza crust

1 tablespoon grated Parmesan

1 cup shredded mozzarella

½ cup diced red onions

1 small tomato, diced

2 tablespoons sliced black olives

½ cup crumbled Asiago

Garnish

2 tablespoons fresh Italian parsley leaves (optional)

Seafood on pizza used to mean anchovies, and I've got a killer recipe for that in this chapter. But I also like smoked salmon, clams, blackened crawfish, and crab. Pairing them with an orange and beet salad, bacon, and pineapple might seem unusual, but wait until you taste the pizzas. And if you think shrimp is ordinary, you haven't tasted my Gamberian pizza. It won first place at Pizza Expo, my highest honor.

Pizzas with Seafood

Acciuga e Porri
Anchovies and sautéed leeks

People who like anchovies usually love them. If you fall into this category, this pizza is for you. It's a big anchovy celebration, where sautéed leeks lend mellowness to the salty fillets. Spanish anchovies are reputed to be among the world's best, although Italians will refute that claim. If possible, buy anchovies packed in salt. They are meatier and have better flavor and texture. Rinse them in water and remove the backbone by peeling it away from the fillet. Soak them in milk for about 30 minutes, so that the lactic acid in the milk cleans out the salt. Pat dry with a paper towel. Salt-packed anchovies may be more trouble, but they are definitely worth the effort. If you use canned anchovies, taste them first. If they are salty or fishy, rinse the fillets well in warm water, and pat them dry.

1 Cut about 3 inches (7½ cm) off the green top of the leek, then slice the leek thinly, lengthwise. Rinse in a colander for several minutes until you see no trace of grit. Place the leek and butter in a medium skillet. Cook on medium heat, stirring often, until the leek softens, about 5 minutes.

2 Brush the grilled side of the pizza crust with the Herbed Grill Oil and dust with the Parmesan. Sprinkle on the mozzarella and Fontina. Pile the leek onto the pizza without spreading. Next, place an anchovy fillet across each pile, and then sprinkle all over with the pepper flakes.

3 Grill the pizza according to Chapter 4. Garnish with the basil leaves before serving.

INGREDIENTS

1 medium leek

1 tablespoon unsalted butter

1 grilled pizza crust

1 tablespoon Herbed Grill Oil (page 28) or extra virgin olive oil

1 tablespoon grated Parmesan

½ cup shredded mozzarella

½ cup shredded Fontina

10 to 12 anchovy fillets

Pinch of crushed pepper flakes

Garnish

2 tablespoons fresh basil leaves, sliced into thin strips

The Arctic Hawaiian
Smoked salmon and tangy glazed pineapple

The concept of opposites that balance each other yet achieve new tastes has always been important in my cooking. An example is the classic Hawaiian pizza of salty ham, complemented by sweet and tart pineapple. My pizza is a twist on the classic with ingredients from opposite climates: smoked Alaskan salmon and fresh Hawaiian pineapple. The pineapple is glazed with honey and mustard and adds contrast and balance to the flavors of salt, sweet, and sour. If you can't find Alaskan cold-smoked salmon, substitute regular smoked salmon.

1 To make the Glazed Pineapple, combine all of the ingredients except the pineapple in a small saucepan on medium-high heat and bring to a boil. Reduce the heat and simmer for a few minutes, until slightly thick and sticky. Add the fresh pineapple and toss to coat completely. Remove from the heat.

2 Brush the grilled side of the pizza crust with the Herbed Grill Oil and dust with the Parmesan. Sprinkle on the mozzarella and add the Glazed Pineapple, red onions, and capers. Tear the smoked salmon into pieces and scatter them evenly on the pizza.

3 Grill the pizza according to Chapter 4. Drizzle with any remaining sauce and garnish with the green onions and the fresh parsley leaves, if desired, before serving.

INGREDIENTS

Glazed Pineapple

4 tablespoons honey

1 teaspoon Dijon mustard

1 tablespoon water

1 tablespoon fresh lemon juice

$1/8$ teaspoon minced fresh ginger

1 cup fresh pineapple, cut into 1-inch (2½ cm) chunks

1 grilled pizza crust

1 tablespoon Herbed Grill Oil (page 28) or extra virgin olive oil

1 tablespoon grated Parmesan

1 cup shredded mozzarella

½ cup thinly sliced red onions

½ teaspoon capers

6 to 8 ounces (175 to 225 g) smoked salmon fillets

Garnish

1 tablespoon thinly sliced green onions

1 tablespoon fresh Italian parsley leaves (optional)

The Ballard Lox
Smoked salmon, arugula, and grape tomatoes

Ballard is a neighborhood in Seattle, Washington, surrounded by Lake Washington. I fished on that lake while on vacation fifteen years ago, and caught several 20-pound (9 kg) King salmon. They were the best I have ever eaten. Ballard is known for its locks, which raise and lower boats so they can continue through the waterways at different elevations. During salmon-spawning season, tourists gather to watch salmon leap through the locks. Do you get my pizza title reference? It's about lox and locks. Arugula pairs well with the saltiness of the salmon and the sweetness of balsamic vinegar. Buy baby arugula because you don't need to chop it into smaller pieces. Freeze the Fontina for a half hour before use to make it easier to shred.

1 Brush the grilled side of the pizza crust with 1 tablespoon of the Herbed Grill Oil. Dust with the Parmesan and sprinkle the mozzarella and Fontina on top.

2 Place the remaining tablespoon of Herbed Grill Oil in a large, deep skillet and heat on high. Throw in the arugula and squeeze the lemon halves over it. Toss the greens quickly, just long enough to wilt them. Immediately transfer to the pizza in small clumps.

3 Roll the salmon slices into small bundles and place them on top of the arugula.

4 Grill the pizza according to Chapter 4. Garnish with the tomatoes and dust with the black pepper before serving, if desired.

INGREDIENTS

1 grilled pizza crust

2 tablespoons Herbed Grill Oil (page 28) or extra virgin olive oil

1 tablespoon grated Parmesan

½ cup shredded mozzarella

½ cup shredded Fontina

4 cups baby arugula, or chopped regular arugula

1 lemon, halved

6 ounces (175 g) thinly sliced smoked salmon

Garnish (optional)

10 grape or small cherry tomatoes, halved and seasoned with salt and pepper

Freshly ground black pepper

Blackened Shrimp Vegas

Shrimp, sausage, and chili con queso

Black and red poker chips were the inspiration for this colorful shrimp pizza with spicy cheese—place your bets on this one! I like Paul Prudhomme's boxed blackening spice mix, found in most supermarkets. I prefer Pace's Thick and Chunky Salsa for this pizza, but any chunky salsa will do.

1 Place the pasteurized cheese and the salsa in a microwave-proof dish or measuring cup. Melt on high for about 2 minutes. Stir together until smooth.

2 Rinse the shrimp under cold running water and pat dry with a paper towel. Toss the shrimp with the blackening spice in a medium bowl, coating them completely. Heat a medium cast-iron skillet or regular sauté pan (do not use nonstick), on high until very hot, about 5 minutes. Turn on the exhaust fan. Add 1 tablespoon of the Herbed Grill Oil. Add the shrimp and sear on one side until blackened, about 2 minutes. Turn them over and take the skillet off the heat. Do not overcook the shrimp.

3 Brush the grilled side of the pizza crust with the remaining tablespoon of Herbed Grill Oil. Dust with the Parmesan and sprinkle with the white Cheddar and Pepper Jack. Drop spoonfuls of the cheese sauce over the pizza without spreading it. Scatter the red onions, green and red peppers, summer sausage, and blackened shrimp over all.

4 Grill the pizza according to Chapter 4. Garnish with the cilantro, if desired, before serving.

INGREDIENTS

4 ounces (100 g) pasteurized, prepared American cheese product, such as Velveeta

½ cup chunky mild salsa

14 peeled and deveined jumbo shrimp

2 tablespoons blackening spice

2 tablespoons Herbed Grill Oil (page 28) or extra virgin olive oil

1 grilled pizza crust

1 tablespoon grated Parmesan

½ cup shredded sharp white Cheddar

½ cup shredded Pepper Jack

½ cup thinly sliced red onions

8 thin circular slices green pepper, about half a pepper

8 thin circular slices red pepper, about half a pepper

14 thin slices summer sausage

Garnish (optional)

¼ cup cilantro, roughly chopped

Clams Casino
Baby clams, roasted peppers, bacon, and Cheddar

The name "Clams Casino" was first coined by Julius Keller, maître d' of the Casino restaurant in Newport, Rhode Island, in 1917. The original dish featured large quahog clams on the half shell, stuffed with bacon, garlic, green or red peppers, and herbed bread crumbs. In the 1950s, it became a popular appetizer made with smaller littleneck clams. Here, I combine all these fixings on a crisp grilled pizza. The creamy sauce adds a bright tomato flavor that complements the bacon, roasted peppers, and, of course, the clams.

1 To make the Creamy Tomato Sauce, place all of the ingredients in a medium bowl and mix well.

2 Brush the grilled side of the pizza crust with the Herbed Grill Oll, dust with the Parmesan, and sprinkle on the mozzarella and Cheddar or Colby. Drop spoonfuls of the Creamy Tomato Sauce onto the pizza. Add the baby clams, bacon, garlic, red onions, and roasted pepper strips.

3 Grill the pizza according to Chapter 4. Garnish with the fresh parsley and pine nuts, if desired, before serving.

INGREDIENTS

Creamy Tomato Sauce

1 cup Chunky Tomato Basil Sauce (page 28)

¼ cup mayonnaise

½ teaspoon Tabasco sauce

½ teaspoon Worcestershire sauce

1 grilled pizza crust

1 tablespoon Herbed Grill Oil (page 28) or extra virgin olive oil

1 tablespoon Parmesan

½ cup shredded mozzarella

½ cup shredded sharp Cheddar or Colby

One 10-ounce (275 g) can baby clams, drained

3 strips bacon, cooked crisp and crumbled

3 cloves garlic, peeled and sliced

½ cup thinly sliced red onions

¼ cup thinly sliced roasted pepper strips (see page 30)

Garnish (optional)

2 tablespoons chopped fresh Italian parsley

1 tablespoon toasted pine nuts

The Gamberian
Sautéed shrimp with pesto and tomato

In 1998, my wife Karla and I were over our heads in debt from our new grilled pizza restaurant in Atlanta, Georgia. One day Karla saw an announcement for an international pizza competition in *Pizza Today*. We knew that winning the contest was the only hope for our struggling new business. My Gamberian won first place at the International Pizza Expo In 1998. By the time we got home, the local media knew we were pizza champs. The next day our phone began ringing nonstop. We happily became accustomed to the feature-length articles praising the ingenuity and culinary attributes of our grilled pizzas, particularly the Gamberian.

1 Brush the grilled side of the pizza crust with 1 tablespoon of the Herbed Grill Oil. Dust with the Parmesan.

2 Heat the remaining tablespoon of oil in a sauté pan over medium heat. Sauté the shrimp until opaque and pink, about 1½ minutes. Don't worry if they seem undercooked; they will cook more when you grill the pizza. Season to taste with salt and black pepper.

3 Top the pizza crust with the mozzarella. Spoon the Chunky Tomato Basil Sauce and the Basil Pecan Pesto on top, creating an alternating pattern of red and green. Add the sun-dried tomatoes, shrimp, red onions, capers, and garlic.

4 Grill the pizza according to Chapter 4. Garnish with the fresh basil and cracked black pepper before serving.

INGREDIENTS

1 grilled pizza crust

2 tablespoons Herbed Grill Oil (page 28) or extra virgin olive oil

1 tablespoon grated Parmesan

½ pound (225 g) jumbo shrimp, shelled and deveined

Salt and freshly ground black pepper

1 cup shredded mozzarella

½ cup Chunky Tomato Basil Sauce (page 28)

½ cup Basil Pecan Pesto (page 30)

¼ cup thinly sliced sun-dried tomatoes (see Note)

½ cup thinly sliced red onions

2 teaspoons capers

3 cloves garlic, thinly sliced

Garnish

2 tablespoons fresh basil leaves, torn

¼ teaspoon cracked black pepper

Note: Buy sun-dried tomatoes packed in olive oil if possible, because they are easier to cut.

The New Orlean

Blackened crawfish, sausage, and spicy apricot sauce

My memories of being a chef in New Orleans inspired this pizza, which won first place in its category at the International Pizza Expo in 1999. The spiciness of the blackened crawfish and the Andouille sausage complements the sweet and tart apricot sauce perfectly. Crawfish tail meat is sold frozen at some fish markets. If you can't find it, substitute frozen rock shrimp. I like Paul Prudhomme's boxed blackening spice mix, found in most supermarkets.

To Save Time: Make the Spicy Apricot Sauce and roast the peppers up to 3 days in advance.

1   To make the Spicy Apricot Sauce, place all of the ingredients in a small saucepan on low heat and stir. Cook until the sauce is slightly thick, stirring often, about 10 minutes. If the sauce becomes so thick that it can't be drizzled, add ½ teaspoon water.

2   Rinse the crawfish under cold running water and pat dry with a paper towel. Toss the crawfish with the blackening spice in a medium bowl until well coated.

3   Heat a medium cast-iron skillet or sauté pan (do not use nonstick) on high until very hot, about 5 minutes. Turn on the exhaust fan. Add 1 tablespoon of the Herbed Grill Oil. Add the crawfish and stir to blacken, about 2 minutes. Add the sausage and sear for a minute or two, until it becomes a little crisp.

4   Brush the grilled side of the pizza crust with the remaining tablespoon of Herbed Grill Oil. Dust with the Parmesan, sprinkle with the mozzarella and Fontina, and top with the crawfish and sausage in an alternating pattern. Add the red onions and the roasted pepper. Drizzle the Spicy Apricot Sauce over all.

5   Grill the pizza according to Chapter 4. Garnish with the cilantro leaves before serving.

INGREDIENTS

Spicy Apricot Sauce

½ cup apricot preserves

1 tablespoon vinegar

1 teaspoon sugar

½ teaspoon chili garlic paste or ½ teaspoon crushed red pepper

Pinch of red pepper flakes

Pinch of salt

¼ pound (100 g) cooked, cleaned crawfish tail meat

1 tablespoon blackening spice mix

2 tablespoons Herbed Grill Oil (page 28) or extra virgin olive oil

¼ pound (100 g) Andouille sausage, about 1½ links, sliced lengthwise and cut into chunks

1 grilled pizza crust

1 tablespoon grated Parmesan

1 cup shredded Mozzarella

½ cup shredded Fontina (see Note)

½ cup thinly sliced red onions

1 roasted red or green pepper (see page 30), cut into strips

Garnish

1 tablespoon cilantro leaves, torn

Note: Freeze the Fontina for a half hour before use to make it easier to shred.

The San Franciscan
Crab with orange and beet salad

When I began working with Dianne, she took me to San Francisco's Ferry Plaza, where we strolled past merchants selling fresh Dungeness crab, flowers, and vegetables. This colorful pizza has the essence of my San Francisco experience: sweet crabmeat, tannic mustard tones, tangy orange sections, and earthy crimson beets. Crushed sourdough pretzels add a salty goodness that reflects San Francisco's famous sourdough bread. Freeze the Fontina cheese for a half hour before use to make it easier to shred.

To Save Time: Make the roasted beet salad up to 3 days in advance, or buy a 2¼-ounce (50 g) can of julienned beets instead.

1 Combine all of the ingredients for the Crab Topping in a small bowl, mix well, and refrigerate.

2 To make the Orange and Beet Salad, preheat the oven to 400°F (200°C). Place the beet on a large piece of aluminum foil and drizzle with the olive oil. Fold up the foil to form a tightly sealed packet, place on a baking sheet, and roast for 1 hour. Pierce the beet with a fork to test for doneness—if the fork goes in easily, the beet is done. Cool for about 15 minutes, or until you can handle. Remove the skin with a paring knife and cut the beet into matchstick strips. Place the beets and the other salad ingredients in a large bowl and toss until well coated.

3 Brush the grilled side of the pizza crust with the Herbed Grill Oil and dust with the Parmesan. Sprinkle with the Fontina or white Cheddar, and drop spoonfuls of the crab topping on top.

4 Grill the pizza according to Chapter 4. Before serving, place spoonfuls of the beet salad on the pizza, and sprinkle the pretzels over all.

INGREDIENTS

Crab Topping

6 ounces (175 g) fresh crabmeat

¼ cup mayonnaise

3 teaspoons Dijon mustard

Juice of ½ lemon

1 teaspoon sugar

2 teaspoons grated Parmesan

2 drops Tabasco sauce

Orange and Beet Salad

1 medium fresh beet

1 teaspoon olive oil

1 can Mandarin orange segments, drained, or 1 cup fresh

1 teaspoon grated lemon zest

2 tablespoons lemon juice

1 teaspoon sugar

¼ teaspoon kosher salt

1 teaspoon olive oil

1 tablespoon fresh chopped dill

2 tablespoons chopped onions

1 grilled pizza crust

1 teaspoon Herbed Grill Oil (page 28) or extra virgin olive oil

1 teaspoon grated Parmesan

1 cup shredded Fontina or white Cheddar

Garnish

2 to 3 large, hard, sourdough pretzels, roughly crumbled

In everything that I cook, I first consider which vegetables to serve. Vegetables are the main flavoring components of any great meal, pizza included. They contribute a rainbow of color and texture. Asparagus, fennel, carrots, broccoli, and many more are so good on a pizza that you won't miss the meat. This chapter also features two classics perfect for kids: the Margheritan, just tomato, basil, and mozzarella; and the Frommagian, a four-cheese pizza.

Pizzas with Vegetables

The Asparago
Asparagus with pesto, pine nuts, and Brie

When cooked long enough, asparagus becomes soft and buttery—so much better than just cooking it until crisp. Searing it caramelizes the skin, which only improves its flavor. The tang of Brie cheese complements this earthy vegetable perfectly.

1 Cut about 2 inches (5 cm) off the ends of the asparagus stems, and then cut into 2-inch (5 cm) pieces. Wash the asparagus under cold running water, and leave wet. The moisture will help steam them in the pan. Sprinkle with salt.

2 Heat 1 tablespoon of the Herbed Grill Oil in a wide skillet on medium-high heat. Add the asparagus pieces and sprinkle again with salt. Sauté briefly for 5 to 7 minutes, depending on the thickness of the asparagus, until it becomes slightly limp.

3 Brush the grilled side of the pizza crust with the remaining tablespoon of Herbed Grill Oil and dust with the Parmesan. Sprinkle with the mozzarella, then drop spoonfuls of the Basil Pecan Pesto onto the pizza. Add the asparagus pieces and lay the slices of Brie beside the asparagus.

4 Grill according to Chapter 4. Garnish with the pine nuts before serving.

INGREDIENTS

1 bunch (about 1 pound/450 g) fresh asparagus

Pinch of salt

2 tablespoons Herbed Grill Oil (page 28) or extra virgin olive oil

1 grilled pizza crust

1 tablespoon grated Parmesan

1 cup shredded mozzarella

½ cup Basil Pecan Pesto (page 30)

4 ounces (100 g) Brie, cut into small slices

Garnish

1 tablespoon pine nuts, toasted

The Aristan

Roasted vegetables with creamy garlic cheese

The word *arist* means "to roast" in Italian. This pizza pairs a variety of roasted vegetables with a base of creamy garlic cheese. Just about any vegetable good for roasting will work, so use what you have on hand. The varying colors and shapes create a striking pizza.

Variation: Try an all-green pizza with broccoli, bok choy, and Swiss chard. Just chop the vegetables into small pieces and roast for 20 minutes.

1 Preheat the oven to 400°F (200°C). To make the roasted vegetables, toss all of the ingredients with the Herbed Grill Oil in a shallow baking dish. Roast until the vegetables are tender and lightly browned, about 25 minutes.

2 Brush the grilled side of the pizza crust with the Herbed Grill Oil. Dust with the Parmesan, and sprinkle with the mozzarella. Spoon the Boursin on top, without spreading it. Pile the roasted vegetables over the pizza.

3 Grill the pizza according to Chapter 4. Garnish with the fennel tops before serving.

INGREDIENTS

Roasted Vegetables

¼ fennel bulb, trimmed and thinly sliced, lengthwise

½ red bell pepper, sliced into thin strips

1 carrot, peeled and sliced ¼ inch thick on the diagonal

½ cup sliced red onions

½ cup broccoli florets

1 portobello mushroom cap, sliced ½ inch (1¼ cm) thick

1 tablespoon fresh rosemary, roughly chopped, or 1 teaspoon dried

½ teaspoon kosher salt

½ teaspoon freshly ground black pepper

1 tablespoon Herbed Grill Oil (page 28) or extra virgin olive oil

1 grilled pizza crust

1 tablespoon Herbed Grill Oil (page 28) or extra virgin olive oil

1 tablespoon grated Parmesan

1 cup shredded mozzarella

One (4.4 ounce/125 g) package Boursin cheese

Garnish

2 tablespoons chopped fennel green tops

The Biancan
Spinach, pesto, mushrooms, and feta

Bianca means "white" in Italian. Traditionally, white pizza has no tomato sauce, so I add Basil Pecan Pesto for a fresh herb flavor. Roasted garlic adds more depth and makes it a vegetarian's favorite pizza.

To save time: Make the roasted garlic up to 3 days in advance.

1 Brush the grilled side of the pizza crust with 1 tablespoon of Herbed Grill Oil. Dust with the Parmesan, and follow with the mozzarella. Drop spoonfuls of the Basil Pecan Pesto onto the pizza, without spreading.

2 Heat the remaining tablespoon of Herbed Grill Oil in a large, deep sauté pan on high. Add the spinach and mushrooms and toss quickly, just long enough to wilt the greens. Drain the vegetables in a colander, pressing out any excess moisture with the back of a large spoon. Season with salt and pepper.

3 Scatter the spinach and mushrooms on the pizza. Add the red onions and garlic cloves. Sprinkle the feta and ricotta over all.

4 Grill the pizza according to Chapter 4.

INGREDIENTS

1 grilled pizza crust

2 tablespoons Herbed Grill Oil (page 28) or extra virgin olive oil

2 tablespoons grated Parmesan

½ cup mozzarella

½ cup Basil Pecan Pesto (page 30)

4 cups fresh spinach, packed

4 large white mushrooms, thinly sliced

Salt and freshly ground black pepper

½ cup thinly sliced red onions

12 whole Roasted Cloves Garlic (page 31)

½ cup crumbled feta

½ cup ricotta

The Fromaggian
Classic four-cheese pizza

Cheese pizzas are comforting and familiar. They remind me of being a kid, when life was about a can of tomato soup and a grilled cheese sandwich on a rainy day. So when you get the urge to simplify, try this pizza for something satisfying. This version has my favorites: mozzarella, Parmesan, white Cheddar, and feta.

Variation: Other cheeses that work well are Fontina, Havarti, smoked Gouda, Jarlsberg, and Gorgonzola.

1 Brush the grilled side of the pizza crust with the Herbed Grill Oil. Dust with the Parmesan, and follow with the mozzarella. Drop spoonfuls of the Chunky Tomato Basil Sauce over the pizza. Finally, top with the white Cheddar and feta.

2 Grill the pizza according to Chapter 4. Garnish with the basil leaves and the parsley, if desired, before serving.

INGREDIENTS

1 grilled pizza crust

1 tablespoon Herbed Grill Oil (page 28) or extra virgin olive oil

1 tablespoon grated Parmesan

½ cup shredded mozzarella

1 cup Chunky Tomato Basil Sauce (page 28)

½ cup shredded white Cheddar

¼ cup crumbled feta cheese

Garnish (optional)

10 fresh basil leaves, torn

1 tablespoon chopped Italian parsley

The Habaneran
Hot peppers with avocado, cilantro, and lime

There was a time when I made and ate grilled pizza every single day. That's when my wife, Karla, and I discovered the habanero pepper. We went crazy over the intensity of the heat. My all-time high was twenty-four habaneros on a 12-inch grilled pizza, two per inch! Karla and I enjoyed watching each other wriggle when hitting an intensely hot bite. I think we drank about six beers each to put out the fire. Here I've added avocado, cilantro, and a squeeze of lime to calm the pizza down. If you enjoy the wonderful agony only the hottest pepper in the world can bring, this is the pizza for you. Start with one and work your way up. It takes a lot of practice and stupidity to get to twenty-four peppers.

1 Brush the grilled side of the pizza crust with the Herbed Grill Oil. Dust with the Parmesan and sprinkle with the mozzarella. Drop spoonfuls of the Chunky Tomato Basil Sauce on top. Finally, throw on some sliced habaneros.

2 Grill the pizza according to Chapter 4. Before serving, garnish with the avocado slices and cilantro, and squeeze the lime juice over all.

INGREDIENTS

1 grilled pizza crust

1 tablespoon Herbed Grill Oil (page 28) or extra virgin olive oil

1 tablespoon grated Parmesan

1 cup shredded mozzarella

1 cup Chunky Tomato Basil Sauce (page 28)

1 to 24 habanero peppers, thinly sliced (see Note)

Garnish

1 avocado, thinly sliced

2 tablespoons cilantro leaves

1 lime, halved

Note: When working with hot chile peppers, do not touch your eyes. Wash your hands, utensils, and cutting board thoroughly as soon as you have finished cutting them.

The Margheritan
Traditional tomato, basil, and cheese

Today's modern pizza of tomato sauce and cheese can be traced back to an Italian pizzario, Raffaele Esposito of Naples, owner of a tavern called Pizzeria di Pietro e Basta Cosi. In 1889, he created a pizza for the visiting Italian King Umberto I and Queen Margherita. He used tomatoes, basil, and mozzarella cheese to represent the Italian flag's colors of red, green, and white. The queen asked Raffaele what the dish was called and the smart chef replied, "The Margherita, after you, my Queen." This recipe calls for two types of mozzarella: One is sold shredded in plastic pouches, available in any supermarket; the other is fresh, a soft, white ball that melts into milky pillows. I usually buy an 8-ounce (225 g) ball called *fior de latte*, or "flowers of milk." Fresh mozzarella has a shelf life of about two weeks.

Variation: Add pepperoni for a stellar spicy pizza.

1 Brush the grilled side of the pizza crust with the Herbed Grill Oil. Dust with the Parmesan and sprinkle with the mozzarella. Drop spoonfuls of the Chunky Tomato Basil Sauce onto the pizza. Tear the fresh mozzarella into chunks and distribute across the pizza, filling in the holes between the sauce.

2 Grill the pizza according to Chapter 4. Garnish with the basil leaves before serving.

INGREDIENTS

1 grilled pizza crust

1 tablespoon Herbed Grill Oil (page 28) or extra virgin olive oil

1 tablespoon grated Parmesan

1 cup shredded mozzarella

½ cup Chunky Tomato Basil Sauce (page 28)

1 ball (8 ounces/225 g) fresh mozzarella

Garnish

2 tablespoons basil leaves

The Verduran

Mixed green vegetables with olives and basil

Verdure is Italian for green, and this mostly green pizza is inspired by that word. If you don't have the exact vegetables listed, substitute others such as zucchini, portobello mushrooms, or artichoke hearts.

1   Brush the grilled side of the pizza crust with the Herbed Grill Oil. Dust with the Parmesan and follow with the mozzarella. Drop spoonfuls of the Chunky Tomato Basil Sauce over the pizza. Place the arugula or spinach over the pizza. Scatter the mushrooms, red onions, peppers, and olives over all.

2   Grill the pizza according to Chapter 4. Garnish with the basil leaves, if desired, before serving.

INGREDIENTS

1 grilled pizza crust

1 tablespoon Herbed Grill Oil (page 28) or extra virgin olive oil

1 tablespoon grated Parmesan

1 cup shredded mozzarella

1 cup Chunky Tomato Basil Sauce (page 28)

1 cup baby arugula or coarsely chopped spinach

1 cup sautéed sliced mushrooms (see page 32)

½ cup thinly sliced red onions

½ cup thinly sliced green or red peppers

2 tablespoons sliced black olives

Garnish (optional)

10 fresh basil leaves, torn

To make piadinas (pee-yah-DEEN-ahs), a popular flatbread sandwich, Italians mix a little flour with water and olive oil, roll out disks of dough, and grill them for a minute on each side. Then they fill them with local foods such as prosciutto, broccoli rabe, and Parmesan. Italians have a saying *"Ogni donna fa la piadina a modo suo."* It means, "Every woman makes piadina in her own special way." Recipes vary as infinitely as the clouds blowing over northern Italy's wheat fields.

Piadinas

Piadina Dough
Traditional unleavened flatbread

This dough is so easy to make and grill that you'll wonder why you haven't made it before. The recipe below gives you the option of making it in a stand mixer, food processor, or by hand, which is my favorite way to get in touch with the dough. A teaspoon of lemon juice is my secret for keeping the dough tender. To make a pizza and piadina for the same meal, save time by making both crusts from pizza dough. Just follow the Piadina Grilling Steps. The piadina will be thicker and a little softer than the traditional unleavened recipe, but will still taste like the best flour tortilla you've ever had. Piadina dough can be made up to 3 days ahead and refrigerated. Once it is rolled out and grilled, wrap the unused portion tightly in plastic wrap and use it within a day. A piadina tastes best when eaten fresh, the same day.

1 **Kneading with a stand mixer:** Measure the flour into a 4- or 5-quart (4–5 liter) bowl. Make a well in the center and pour in the salt, olive oil, water, and lemon juice. Use the dough hook attachment (mine is shaped like an S, but I've seen others shaped like a C) on the lowest speed to allow the ingredients to come together. Move to medium-high speed and knead for about 5 minutes. The finished dough should form a ball, unless it's too wet or sticky. If so, add flour by the ½ teaspoon until the dough comes off the sides cleanly and forms a ball.

Kneading with a food processor: Use the plastic blade made especially for dough (the metal blade can tear the dough to pieces). Place all of the ingredients into the bowl. Use a pulse action until the dough comes together. Continue to pulse the dough in quick bursts for about 3 minutes. This technique keeps the dough from overheating.

INGREDIENTS

1½ cups unbleached flour

½ teaspoon salt

2 tablespoons extra virgin olive oil, plus 1 teaspoon for oiling the dough

½ cup water

1 teaspoon lemon juice

Makes 4 piadinas

TIP

Why knead?

I can't prove that piadinas taste better when a cook touches the dough, but I always knead by hand. I use the machine for the first part, just until the dough comes together. Then I remove the ball, slap it on the counter, and pour all my energy and affection into kneading. Some of what I work into the dough transfers to the finished product. I like to think that my family and guests feel the love.

Kneading by hand: Measure the flour into a large bowl and make a well in the center. Pour the salt, olive oil, water, and lemon juice into the well. Mix well, stirring with a strong spoon. The finished dough should form a ball, unless it's too wet or sticky. (If so, add tiny amounts of flour, until the dough comes off the sides cleanly and forms a ball.) Lightly flour a clean, dry countertop. Place the ball of dough on the counter, and press down with the palm of your hand. Fold the dough over itself and press again. Continue to roll and press the dough for about 8 minutes, or until the dough Is smooth. You will feel the dough change. It will soften and become more elastic. Add only enough flour to prevent it from sticking.

2 When the dough is ready, it will be soft, smooth, and firm. Lightly oil the ball of dough with olive oil. Wrap it in plastic and let it rest for about 30 minutes. This resting period allows the gluten to relax, creating soft, tender dough that is easier to roll out.

3 Cut the dough into 4 equal pieces. Roll them into rounds about 8 inches (20 cm) in diameter. Follow the Piadina Grilling Steps on pages 120–121 to finish.

Jalapeño Piadina Dough
Green flatbread with a kick

The gentle heat and soft green color from the jalapeños and cilantro make these piadinas irresistible. They go well with vegetarian sandwiches such as the Piadina Radicchio (page 134), or with some strips of freshly grilled steak.

Note: When working with hot chile peppers, do not touch your eyes. Wash your hands, utensils, and cutting board thoroughly as soon as you have finished.

1 Place the peppers in a blender or food processor with the cilantro, water, and lemon juice and blend until smooth.

2 Add the flour, salt, and olive oil. Follow the remaining instructions as per the Piadina Dough recipe at left.

INGREDIENTS

12 slices (from 5-ounce/150 g can) sliced jalapeño chile peppers, drained thoroughly

1 tablespoon chopped cilantro leaves

¼ cup water

1 teaspoon lemon juice

1½ cups unbleached flour

½ teaspoon salt

2 tablespoons extra virgin olive oil, plus 1 teaspoon for oiling the dough

Makes 4 piadinas

Tomato Basil Piadina Dough
Red and green speckled flatbread

This piadina dough brings a fresh Italian flavor to your sandwich. It's also attractive, with its red hue and bright green flecks.

1 **Kneading with a stand mixer:** Follow the technique on page 116. Add the tomato paste and basil into the well.

   Kneading with a food processor: Follow the technique on page 116.

   Kneading by hand: Follow the technique on page 117. Add the tomato paste and basil into the well.

2 See page 117, Step 2, for further instruction.

3 Cut the dough into 4 equal pieces. Roll them into rounds about 8 inches (20 cm) in diameter. Follow the Piadina Grilling Steps on pages 120–121 to finish.

INGREDIENTS

1½ cups unbleached flour

¼ cup, plus 2 tablespoons water

2 tablespoons extra virgin olive oil, plus 1 teaspoon for oiling the dough

1 teaspoon salt

3 ounces (75 g) tomato paste

¼ cup chopped fresh basil leaves

Makes 4 piadinas

Yellow Corn Piadina Dough
Chewy yellow flatbread

Making piadina dough with yellow cornmeal adds a pleasant chewiness and a flavor that pairs well with Italian-inspired fillings.

1 **Kneading with a stand mixer:** Measure the flour, cornmeal, and salt into a 4- or 5-quart (4 or 5 liter) bowl. Pulse briefly to mix. Make a well in the center and add the sugar, melted butter, lemon juice, and water. See page 116 for further instruction.

Kneading with a food processor: Follow the technique on page 116.

Kneading by hand: Put the flour, cornmeal, and salt into a mixing bowl and stir to combine. Make a well in the center and add the sugar, melted butter, lemon juice, and water in the well.

2 See page 117, Step 2, for further instruction.

3 Cut the dough into 6 equal pieces. Roll them into rounds about 8 inches (20 cm) in diameter. Follow the Piadina Grilling Steps on pages 120–121 to finish.

INGREDIENTS

1 cup unbleached flour

½ cup yellow cornmeal

1 teaspoon salt

2 teaspoons sugar

2 tablespoons melted unsalted butter

1 teaspoon lemon juice

½ cup water

Makes 4 piadinas

Piadina Grilling Steps

About 500 years ago in Italy, peasants once laid piadina dough on a stone heated over a wood fire for about a minute. Today, you can use an outdoor or indoor grill on high heat, or cook the piadina on indoor surfaces such as a flat griddle, skillet, or cast-iron frying pan on medium-high heat. You'll be surprised by how quickly the piadina is ready. Grilling only takes a few minutes.

1 Heat the cooking surface until it is extremely hot. Test with a drop of water, which will sputter across the surface and quickly disappear, and the surface will smoke lightly. Lay the dough rounds on the hot surface. If the surface is hot enough, the dough will not stick. If it does, remove the dough and spray the cooking surface lightly with vegetable oil, or moisten a crumpled paper towel with a drop of vegetable oil and wipe the surface of the grill.

2 Cook the dough for about 1 minute, or until bubbles form on the surface.

Storage: Refrigerate extra piadinas for up to 3 days by wrapping them tightly in plastic wrap and slipping them into a plastic bag. Avoid freezing, as they tend to dry out. To reheat, place in the microwave for about 10 seconds on high.

3 Lift the piadina with tongs to check its doneness. The cooked side should have charred little bubbles. Turn the piadina over, and cook for another minute, until the bottom is light brown.

4 Stack the cooked piadinas on a clean towel and wrap them so they stay warm. For best results, serve within 30 minutes of cooking.

Piadina Dolce e Salato

Soppressata with Parmesan crisps and honey

Dolce e salato means "sweet and salty" in Italian. Honey has added flavor to ham for centuries, since its sweetness brings out the saltiness of the meat. These two flavors come together here, where spicy soppressata and honey pair with Parmesan for triple the pleasure.

1 Preheat the oven to 400°F (200°C). To make the Parmesan crisps, pour a heaping tablespoon of Parmesan onto a silicone or parchment paper–lined baking sheet. Pat it down lightly. Repeat with the remaining cheese, spacing the spoonfuls about ½ inch (12 mm) apart. Bake for 3 to 5 minutes or until golden and crisp. Let cool.

2 Place each piadina on a plate. Smear 3 garlic cloves on each, using a butter knife. Follow with 2 lettuce leaves on one side, half the cheese crisps, 3 tomato slices, then half the soppressata, folding the slices in half as you lay them down.

3 Drizzle 1 tablespoon of the honey onto each sandwich filling. Season with pepper. Fold each piadina in half and serve.

INGREDIENTS

½ cup grated Parmesan

2 freshly made piadinas

6 Roasted Garlic Cloves (page 31)

4 leaves Romaine lettuce

6 thin slices tomato

4 ounces (100 g) thinly sliced soppressata, 8 to 10 slices

2 tablespoons honey

Freshly ground black pepper

Makes 2 piadinas

Piadina Firenze
Eggplant and peppers with tomato vinaigrette

Smoky grilled eggplant is the featured filling of this vegetarian piadina, brightened by a tomato vinaigrette, roasted red peppers, and salty Parmesan.

1 Prepare a grill for direct grilling over high heat.

2 Cut the eggplant into six round slices. Place the slices in a bowl, sprinkle with the salt, and toss to coat. Let sit for about 15 minutes.

3 To make the Tomato Vinaigrette, place the diced tomato in a medium bowl. Add the olive oil, balsamic vinegar, and parsley and season with salt and pepper. Mix thoroughly.

4 Rinse the eggplant slices in cold running water and pat them dry with paper towels. Place in a bowl and add the tablespoon of olive oil. Toss the eggplant until well coated.

5 Grill the red pepper about 2 minutes per side, or until black on all sides. While the pepper cooks, place the eggplant slices on the grill and cook for about 3 minutes on each side, until they look slightly soft. Remove from the heat and cool slightly. Peel the skin off each slice, if desired.

6 Remove the roasted pepper from the heat, place in a bowl, and cover with a towel or plastic wrap for 5 minutes. Remove the blackened peel and seeds and cut into strips.

7 Place each piadina on a plate. Place 2 leaves of lettuce on one half of each piadina. Add 3 eggplant slices and half the roasted red pepper strips, then spoon the Tomato Vinaigrette over all. Add the Parmesan and a few grinds of pepper. Fold each piadina in half and serve.

INGREDIENTS

1 small eggplant

1 teaspoon salt

Tomato Vinaigrette

1 small tomato, diced (about ¼ cup)

2 tablespoons extra virgin olive oil

1 tablespoon balsamic vinegar

1 tablespoon chopped fresh Italian parsley

Salt and freshly ground black pepper

1 tablespoon extra virgin olive oil

1 red pepper

2 freshly made piadinas

4 leaves romaine lettuce

2 ounces (50 g) shaved Parmesan

Freshly ground black pepper

Makes 2 piadinas

Piadina Genovese

Grilled chicken with pesto, pine nuts, and olives

Italians love antipasti, those small portions of meats, cheeses, olives, and peppers served before a main course. A classic antipasto is a chicken breast smothered in pesto. Try it inside a piadina and make a whole meal of it. For an old-school Italian touch, toss in a few anchovies, which add salt and a rich, briny flavor that blends in without tasting fishy.

1 Mix the lemon juice and Basil Pecan Pesto in a small bowl.

2 Place each piadina on a plate. Place 2 leaves of lettuce on one side of each piadina, then top with half the grilled chicken slices. Drizzle 1 tablespoon of the Basil Pecan Pesto over the chicken. (If the sauce is too thick, add a drop of water to thin.)

3 Top each piadina with half the red onion, pine nuts, Parmesan, olives, and anchovies, if desired. Season with the pepper. Fold in half to serve.

INGREDIENTS

2 teaspoons lemon juice

2 tablespoons Basil Pecan Pesto (page 30)

2 freshly made piadinas

4 leaves romaine lettuce

One 6-ounce (175 g) Grilled Chicken Breast (page 29), sliced

2 slices red onion

1 tablespoon toasted pine nuts (see page 29)

2 tablespoons grated Parmesan

8 Kalamata olives, pitted

4 anchovy fillets (optional)

Freshly ground black pepper

Makes 2 piadinas

Piadina Milano
Hard salami with greens and fried eggs

Salami fried in a pan is salami on steroids, where flavors become more concentrated. Add eggs fried in butter and melted cheese—a traditional Milanese combination—and you have one terrific piadina. Bel Paese is a semi-soft cheese with a mild, buttery flavor, which melts beautifully.

1   In a large skillet over medium heat, fry the salami slices about a minute on each side, just until they get hot. Remove from the skillet and set aside.

2   Add the butter to the same pan and crack the eggs into the pan. Fry the eggs to your liking. (Over-easy eggs take about 1 minute per side, medium-firm yolks take about 2 minutes per side, and 4 minutes on each side gives you firm, well-done eggs.)

3   Place each piadina on a plate. Spread 1 teaspoon of the mustard on one side of each piadina. Toss half the greens on top, then add three slices of salami and two of the eggs. Season with salt and pepper, and add the cheese. Fold in half and serve.

INGREDIENTS

6 slices Genoa salami

1 teaspoon unsalted butter

4 large eggs

2 freshly made piadinas

2 teaspoons stone ground mustard

1 cup shredded bitter greens, such as spinach, endive, or romaine lettuce

Salt and freshly ground black pepper

½ cup shredded Asiago, Fontina, or Bel Paese

Makes 2 piadinas

Piadina Mortadella
Italian deli meat with olive relish

Mortadella, an Italian deli meat similar to American bologna (but better), originated near Bologna in the Emilia-Romagna region of Italy. To make it, fresh cuts of pork and ground meat are combined with myrtle berries, nutmeg, and coriander, then ground into a paste and studded with bits of pork fat. It is worth the expense to buy imported mortadella instead of domestic, unless you can find one made by an artisan producer. You'll notice the difference. The Olive Relish adds crunch and a more complex taste, and only takes a moment to make.

To save time: Make the Olive Relish one day in advance.

1 To make the Olive Relish, combine all of the ingredients in a medium bowl and mix well. Let sit, covered, for about an hour, so the flavors blend.

2 Place each piadina on a plate. Lay two lettuce leaves on one side of each piadina. Add half the mortadella, folding the slices in half as you lay them down. Add some of the Olive Relish and half of the shaved Parmesan. Fold each piadina in half and serve with any remaining Olive Relish on the side, if desired.

INGREDIENTS

Olive Relish

1 small tomato, diced (about ¼ cup)

½ cup chopped green olives with pimentos

¼ cup toasted walnut pieces (see page 29)

¼ cup finely chopped celery

2 tablespoons extra virgin olive oil

½ teaspoon sugar

Freshly ground black pepper

2 freshly made piadinas

4 leaves romaine lettuce

4 ounces (100 g) thinly sliced mortadella, 8 to 10 slices

½ cup shaved Parmesan

Makes 2 piadinas

Piadina Neapolitan
Grilled cheese with tomato and basil

This Italian grilled cheese sandwich, with its crisp, golden crust, is my favorite savory piadina. The combination of fresh mozzarella, ripe tomato, and fresh basil is famous throughout Italy, particularly in Naples, where it originated. The three colors represent the Italian flag. Use the highest quality ingredients you can find: fragrant, ripe tomatoes; the best extra virgin olive oil; and fresh mozzarella that melts into milky pillows. I usually buy an 8-ounce (225 g) ball called *fior de latte*, or "flowers of milk," though some delis sell the cheese in smaller balls. It has a shelf life of about two weeks.

1 Place each piadina on a plate. Lay 2 slices of mozzarella on one side of each piadina. Add 3 basil leaves and 2 slices of tomato. Season with salt and pepper, then fold in half. Brush the top of each piadina crust with olive oil.

2 Heat a medium skillet or griddle over medium-high heat. Place each piadina in the pan, oiled side down. Brush the top halves with olive oil.

3 Press down on the piadinas with a spatula while they cook, about 2 minutes. Turn the sandwich over. It should be golden and crisp on the outside. Continue pressing down, about 2 minutes more, until the cheese inside is melted. Remove from the heat and serve immediately.

INGREDIENTS

2 freshly made Tomato Basil piadinas (page 118)

4 slices fresh mozzarella (about 4 ounces/100 g)

6 large basil leaves

4 slices tomato

Kosher salt and freshly ground black pepper

2 tablespoons extra virgin olive oil

Makes 2 piadinas

The PAT Piadina
Pancetta, Arugula, and Tomato

Pancetta is Italian bacon made of cured pork belly. Unlike American bacon, it is not smoked. Instead, its flavor comes from salted and spiced meat. Many Italian dishes, including soups, pastas, and vegetable dishes, are flavored with pancetta. I love it as the star of this piadina. The contrast of crisp and hot pancetta, creamy pesto mayonnaise, and cool tomato and arugula can't be beat. Sliced pancetta, available at delis, looks like rounds of meat. When fried, it comes unraveled and looks more like bacon.

1 Heat the olive oil in a large heavy skillet over medium heat. Work in two batches, and fry the pancetta until crisp, about 5 minutes for each batch. Drain on paper towels.

2 Combine the mayonnaise with the Basil Pecan Pesto.

3 Place each piadina on a plate. Spread half the pesto mayonnaise on each piadina. Place half the tomato slices on one half of each piadina. Heap the arugula on top, then half the pancetta. Season with pepper, fold, and serve immediately.

INGREDIENTS

1 tablespoon extra virgin olive oil

3 ounces (75 g) thinly sliced pancetta

2 tablespoons mayonnaise

1 teaspoon Basil Pecan Pesto (page 30)

2 freshly made piadinas

4 slices tomato

2 cups baby arugula

Freshly ground black pepper

Makes 2 piadinas

Piadina Radicchio
Bitter greens, roasted garlic, and Gorgonzola

This deeply flavored sandwich blends salty, smoky, crunchy, and creamy tastes. Grilling the radicchio mellows its slightly bitter flavors. Cultivation of radicchio dates back to the fifteenth century, when it was a small head of green leaves. Three centuries later, a Belgian agronomist used a whitening technique to create the red leaves and white veins we see in today's radicchio, which is rich in an enzyme that purifies the blood and liver. It's also high in antioxidants and a great cancer fighter. Choose radicchio with crisp, full-colored leaves with no wilting or browning—and enjoy these piadinas in good health.

To save time: Make the dressing up to 1 day in advance.

1 Combine all the Balsamic Vinaigrette ingredients, except the balsamic vinegar, in a small bowl and mix well. Add the balsamic vinegar and mix until smooth. Chill, covered, for 15 minutes to let the flavors come together.

2 Cut the head of the radicchio in half, and the halves into quarters lengthwise. Drizzle with the olive oil and season with a pinch of salt. Place on a hot grill on direct heat, or in a medium skillet or griddle, and sear for about 2 minutes on each side, until it is brown and slightly wilted. Remove from the heat, and cut off the white part on the bottom.

3 Place each piadina on a plate. Spread 3 cloves of garlic on each, using a butter knife. Place half of the lettuce, tomato slices, and radicchio on one half of each piadina. Sprinkle with the walnuts and Gorgonzola, then drizzle with the Balsamic Vinaigrette. Fold in half and serve.

INGREDIENTS

Balsamic Vinaigrette

1½ teaspoons Dijon mustard

2 tablespoons minced onions

Zest of 1 lemon

2 tablespoons lemon juice

¼ teaspoon celery seeds

1½ tablespoons extra virgin olive oil

½ teaspoon sugar

¼ teaspoon salt

¼ teaspoon freshly ground black pepper

1 tablespoon balsamic vinegar

1 small head radicchio, about the size of an orange

2 tablespoons extra virgin olive oil

Pinch of salt

2 freshly made piadinas

6 Roasted Garlic Cloves (page 31)

2 tablespoons crumbled 1 cup shredded romaine lettuce

4 slices tomato

2 tablespoons roughly chopped walnuts, toasted (page 29)

2 tablespoons crumbled Gorgonzola

Makes 2 piadinas

Piadina Romagna
Traditional prosciutto and cheese

This is the most traditional way to eat a piadina: just prosciutto, cheese, and olive oil. The Italians have eaten them this way in the Emilia-Romagna region for centuries.

1 Place each piadina on a plate. Put half of the prosciutto on one half of each piadina, and sprinkle with the Romano. Drizzle the olive oil over both halves.

2 Season with pepper, fold, and serve.

INGREDIENTS

2 freshly made piadinas

3 ounces (75 g) prosciutto, about 9 slices

2 ounces thinly shaved Romano

1 tablespoon extra virgin olive oil

Freshly ground black pepper

Makes 2 piadinas

Piadina Saraceno
Italian sausage with peppers, onions, and mushrooms

The ancient Saraceno market in Bologna has been a vibrant place of exchange and commerce since the early 1500s. The villagers hold grand fairs that honor certain traditions, one of the oldest of which is the Cured Meat and Cheese Fair, held annually in May. This is my kind of event, where more than a hundred vendors sell the best pork sausages and cheeses of the region, and pour generous glasses of local wine. I honor this festival with a juicy piadina of sausage and cheese, laced with pan-roasted peppers, onions, and mushrooms.

1 Heat the olive oil in a medium skillet over medium-high heat. Brown the sausage for about 3 minutes on one side. Turn them over. Add the onions, peppers, and mushrooms and cover. Reduce the heat to medium, and cook for about 10 minutes, stirring occasionally, until the sausage and vegetables are cooked through. Remove the sausage and slice in half lengthwise.

2 Place each piadina on a plate. Put half the Parmesan on one half of each piadina, then top with half the vegetables and sausage slices. Squeeze a lemon wedge over all and season with pepper. Fold in half and serve.

INGREDIENTS

1 tablespoon extra virgin olive oil

8 ounces (225 g) raw Italian pork sausage (about 2 sausages)

½ cup sliced onions

½ cup thinly sliced red peppers

1 cup sliced fresh mushrooms

2 freshly made piadinas

½ cup shaved Parmesan

2 wedges of lemon

Freshly ground black pepper

Makes 2 pladinas

The perfect accompaniment to grilled pizzas is a cool, crispy salad. The secret is knowing how to match the taste. To help you out, I give pairing suggestions before every recipe. Most of these salads are my own creation. Even with a classic Caesar, I add a little twist. And some are robust enough to be entrees. The crowning touch comes when presenting these salads in a bowl made from a pizza shell. It's so easy to make that you won't believe it.

Salads

The Bakery Bowl
A crispy pizza crust for salads

Impress your guests with this easy salad bowl made from pizza crust. The dough bakes in the oven, draped over a bowl, and creates a pretty rim that looks like flower petals. When you fill it with salad (see page 154), it makes a dramatic yet fun presentation—and it's tasty to boot.

1   Preheat the oven to 450°F (230°C). Dust your counter with a light sprinkle of flour. Place the dough on the counter and dust the top with a little extra flour. Roll it out to about a 12-inch (30 cm) circle, keeping the dough as even as possible.

2   Poke the dough a few times with the tines of a fork to prevent it from blowing up into a ball. This is called "docking the dough."

3   Turn the bowl over and place it on a baking sheet. Use a pastry brush, spray oil, or moisten a crumpled paper towel with a drop of vegetable oil to coat the dough completely—the dough will stick to any surface that is not well oiled. Sprinkle the outer surface of the bowl evenly with cornmeal. Spread the dough over the bowl and let the edges fall evenly around it so that it surrounds the bowl and creates a draped rim. If it bunches up a little here and there around the edges, leave it. The rustic appearance looks artistic. Do not press down on the dough or it may stick to the bowl.

4   Place the dough bowl, still on the baking sheet, in the oven. Bake for 10 to 15 minutes, until it is browned and puffy. Remove the bowl from the oven and let it cool for about 5 minutes. Carefully pick up the bowl and remove the crust, then place the bread bowl on the counter to cool a little more. Brush the rim with the Herbed Grill Oil. Fill with salad and serve.

INGREDIENTS

Flour for dusting

½ recipe grilled pizza dough (see page 22)

One 1-quart (1 liter) ovenproof bowl, preferably stainless steel

Spray vegetable oil, or 1 tablespoon vegetable oil

1 tablespoon cornmeal, preferably white

1 tablespoon Herbed Grlll Oil (page 28), extra virgin olive oil, or unsalted butter

Makes 1 bread bowl

TIP

Try it with soup
To fill the Bakery Bowl with your favorite soup, put a real bowl inside the Bakery Bowl in case it springs a leak. Thick soups such as bean and minestrone work best. You can even try it with chili or beef stew.

Antipasto Pasta Salad
Antipasti with a sweet basil vinaigrette

The Italian antipasti of meats, olives, and roasted peppers, served before the meal, stimulates the appetite for what follows. In fact, *antipasti* literally means "before the meal." This salad is inspired by that idea, with a colorful topping of salami, red peppers, Kalamata olives, and tomato. It's best served with Italian pizzas such as the Vesuvian (page 83), with chicken and roasted potatoes; the Parma e Fiche (page 60), with figs, prosciutto, and Gorgonzola; or the Emilian (page 52), with prosciutto and cantaloupe chutney.

Variation: If you have leftover Basil Pecan Pesto (page 30), toss it with the pasta before adding it to the salad. The result is a salad with a deeper flavor.

To save time: Make the dressing up to 3 days in advance.

1 Combine the Sweet Basil Vinaigrette ingredients in a small bowl and mix well. Chill for 30 minutes to let the flavors come together.

2 Place the cooked pasta, lettuce, and red onions in a large bowl or Bakery Bowl (page 140), and toss with the Sweet Basil Vinaigrette. Add the salami, roasted red peppers, olives, and tomato. Sprinkle with the Parmesan and serve.

INGREDIENTS

Sweet Basil Vinaigrette

1 tablespoon chopped basil leaves or 1 teaspoon dried basil

1 clove garlic, minced

2 tablespoons extra virgin olive oil

1½ tablespoons red wine vinegar

1 teaspoon sugar

⅛ teaspoon salt

⅛ teaspoon freshly ground black pepper

1 cup cooked rotini pasta, about 2½ ounces (62 g) dry

3 cups chopped romaine lettuce

½ cup thinly sliced red onions

8 slices salami, cut into strips

¼ cup thin strips of roasted red peppers (see page 30)

8 to 9 Kalamata olives

1 small tomato, diced (about ¼ cup)

1 tablespoon grated Parmesan

Makes 2 to 3 servings as a side salad

Curried Carrot Raisin Salad

Carrot, jicama, and apple in a curry dressing

Here's an old Southern favorite, updated with curry powder and lemon and orange. The recipe calls for plain yogurt, but you can substitute mayonnaise for a creamier, but less tangy, salad. Because of its sweetness and bright tones, this salad is a cool accompaniment to the spicier pizzas, such as the Texan (page 77), with barbecued chicken, or the Buffalo Wing (page 70) with blue cheese and celery.

To save time: Make the dressing up to 3 days in advance.

1 To prepare the Curry Dressing, place the sugar, sesame oil, and olive oil in a wide skillet. Heat on high, stirring constantly for 2 to 3 minutes, or until the sugar melts. Add the curry powder and stir. If the sugar starts to solidify, don't worry. It will liquefy as it cooks.

2 Turn down the heat to medium. Add the vinegar, orange juice, raisins, lemon zest, salt, black pepper, and red pepper flakes. Stir and reduce for about 5 minutes over medium heat, until it is thick like honey. Keep a close eye on it to keep it from burning.

3 Pour the sauce into a small bowl. Chill for 15 minutes to let the flavors come together. Add the yogurt and mix well.

4 Shave the carrot, jicama, and apple into thin strips with a box grater. Alternatively, grate the vegetables in a food processor, if you have the grating wheel. Sprinkle the lemon juice over the apple to prevent it from darkening. Mix the vegetables and apple together in a medium bowl. Add the Curry Dressing. Garnish with the cilantro and serve.

INGREDIENTS

Curry Dressing

¼ cup sugar

1½ teaspoons dark sesame oil

1 tablespoon extra virgin olive oil

1½ teaspoons curry powder

2 tablespoons apple cider vinegar

½ cup orange juice

¼ cup dark raisins

Zest of ½ lemon

¼ teaspoon salt

Pinch of black pepper

Pinch of red pepper flakes

¼ cup plain yogurt

1 large carrot

½ small jicama (about the size of a navel orange), peeled

½ red apple, preferably Fuji or Gala

1 tablespoon lemon juice

Garnish

1 tablespoon chopped cilantro

Makes 2 to 3 servings as a side salad

Escarole Siciliano
Crisp and simple escarole with lemon

Escarole is one of my favorite lettuces. It's slightly bitter, a little chewy, and delightfully crisp. If you've never bought it before, it looks like a big, flattened butter lettuce. Because of its great flavor and texture, escarole tastes best ice cold, with minimal interference. All you need is a little oil, red wine vinegar, and lemon to brighten it up. This salad tastes particularly good with the Margheritan grilled pizza (page 110), for a simple but perfect meal of classics. The Vesuvian (page 83), with its sautéed chicken, roasted potatoes, and olives, also complements it well.

1 Remove the lettuce's core with a paring knife. Tear the escarole into bite-sized pieces and rinse under cold running water. Use a salad spinner, if you have one, to spin the lettuce dry, or pat it dry with paper towels.

2 Put the lettuce in a large bowl and chill in the refrigerator for 15 minutes, to get it good and crisp.

3 Drizzle on the oil and vinegar. Add the lemon juice and season with salt and pepper. Toss until evenly coated. Serve in a Bakery Bowl (page 140), if desired.

INGREDIENTS

1 head escarole lettuce (about 5 cups)

2 tablespoons extra virgin olive oil

1 tablespoon red wine vinegar

1½ teaspoons lemon juice

¼ teaspoon kosher salt

¼ teaspoon freshly ground black pepper

Makes 2 to 3 servings as a side salad

Fatoosh Salad
Pizza crust and romaine with a spicy vinaigrette

Fatoosh is a Middle Eastern salad made with leftover pita bread, dressed with a simple lemon vinaigrette. This one uses pieces of grilled pizza crust, a terrific way to use up extra dough. Traditionally, the dressing includes sumac, which adds a reddish color and a spicy taste. Sumac is not always easy to find, so here I've used cumin and paprika, spices more likely to be in your pantry. Serve this salad with the Moroccan (page 74), a curried honey and chicken pizza; or the Aristan (page 105), with its garlicky collection of roasted vegetables.

To save time: Make the dressing up to 3 days in advance.

1 Place the Lemon Vinaigrette ingredients in a small bowl and mix well. Chill for 15 minutes to let the flavors come together.

2 Roll out the pizza dough according to page 26. Grill the pizza crust according to Chapter 4, but grill the crust on both sides while basting it with olive oil. It should be thin and crisp when you are done.

3 Break the pizza crust into bite-sized pieces and place in a large bowl. Add the lettuce, cucumber, tomatoes, green onions, parsley, and mint and toss to combine.

4 Pour the Lemon Vinaigrette over the salad, toss well, and serve.

INGREDIENTS

Lemon Vinaigrette

2 cloves garlic, chopped

½ teaspoon ground cumin

Zest of 1 lemon

¼ cup fresh lemon juice

¼ cup extra virgin olive oil

½ teaspoon salt

½ teaspoon paprika

1 teaspoon sugar

¼ teaspoon black pepper

½ recipe pizza dough

2 tablespoons extra virgin olive oil for basting crust

2 cups chopped romaine lettuce

1 cup chopped cucumber

½ cup diced tomatoes

¼ cup chopped green onions

¼ cup chopped fresh Italian parsley

¼ cup chopped fresh mint

Makes 2 to 3 servings as a side salad

Grapefruit Caesar

A classic salad gets an update

This simple twist on a classic Caesar uses red grapefruit instead of croutons. You'll be delighted with the salad's flavor, color, elegance, and simplicity. Since some people are wary of eating the raw egg in a traditional Caesar dressing, I've replaced it with a little mayonnaise, which also makes for a creamier dressing. I've omitted anchovies, but if you like them, top this with several slices. Or add half an anchovy, chopped, to the dressing. This salad is perfect with the Gamberian grilled pizza (page 95), with its shrimp, tomato sauce, and pesto; or the New Orlean (page 96).

To save time: Make this dressing up to 3 days in advance.

1 Place the Caesar Dressing ingredients in a small bowl and mix well. Chill for 15 minutes to let the flavors come together.

2 Meanwhile, remove the core from the lettuce with a paring knife. Tear the lettuce into bite-sized pieces and rinse under cold running water. Use a salad spinner, if you have one, to spin the lettuce dry, or pat it dry with paper towels.

3 Place the lettuce in a large bowl or Bakery Bowl (page 140) and toss it with the dressing. Add the grapefruit sections, sprinkle with the Parmesan, add a few grinds of black pepper, and serve.

INGREDIENTS

Caesar Dressing

1 clove garlic, minced

1 tablespoon mayonnaise

1 tablespoon red vinegar

1 teaspoon Dijon mustard

½ teaspoon Worcestershire sauce

½ teaspoon sugar

⅛ teaspoon salt

1 tablespoon fresh lemon juice

3 tablespoons extra virgin olive oil

1 medium head Romaine lettuce (about 5 cups)

1 seedless red grapefruit, peeled and split into sections

2 tablespoons grated Parmesan

Freshly ground black pepper

Makes 2 to 3 servings as a side salad

The Greek
The traditional salad with sweet basil vinaigrette

The Greek was the only salad we served at my restaurant. People liked its colorful red tomatoes and peppers, black olives, white feta, and crisp green vegetables. Plus, it's chock-full of healthy ingredients that go well together. But the real reason they ordered this Greek salad is because it tastes so good. The basil lends a little sweetness to balance the saltiness of the feta and olives. The crunchy cucumber and crisp lettuce will keep you coming back for more. To keep the Greek theme, serve this salad with the Olympian (page 59), with sausage and pepperoni; or the Millennium (page 56), with ground lamb.

To save time: Make the dressing up to 3 days in advance.

1 Place the lettuce in a large bowl or Bakery Bowl (page 140). Toss in the red onions, cucumber, red peppers, and olives.

2 Sprinkle the feta over all and place the tomato all around the edge. Add the pepperoncini peppers, pour the Sweet Basil Vinaigrette over the salad, and serve.

INGREDIENTS

3 cups chopped romaine lettuce

¼ cup thinly sliced red onions

6 slices cucumber

¼ cup thinly sliced red peppers

½ cup sliced green or Kalamata olives, or a combination

¼ cup crumbled feta

1 small tomato, diced (about ¼ cup)

3 pepperoncini peppers

1 recipe Sweet Basil Vinaigrette (page 142)

Makes 2 to 3 servings as a side salad

Maytag Blue Chicken Salad
Chicken, blue cheese, and bacon

This hearty and colorful salad can be the entrée that follows a pizza appetizer, or a great side dish for a grilled pizza or piadina party. Its sweet and tangy paprika dressing laces the grilled chicken, crisp greens, avocado, tomato, and Maytag blue cheese. Made by Maytag Dairy Farms outside Newton, Iowa, Maytag is produced by hand and aged in caves, which results in an exceptional quality: salty, earthy, and milky. If you cannot find Maytag blue cheese, substitute any blue-veined cheese. This salad goes well with the classic and simple Margheritan (page 110).

To save time: Make the dressing up to 3 days in advance.

1 Place the Sweet Paprika Dressing ingredients a small bowl and mix well. Chill for 15 minutes to let the flavors come together.

2 Meanwhile, cut the core from the radicchio and slice it thinly. Dry well with a paper towel or in a salad spinner.

3 Toss the radicchio and lettuce with half of the dressing in a large bowl or Bakery Bowl (page 140). Top with all the other ingredients and drizzle the rest of the dressing on top. Add a few grinds of pepper and serve.

INGREDIENTS

Sweet Paprika Dressing

¼ cup mayonnaise

½ zest of 1 lime

1 tablespoon lime juice

1½ teaspoons red wine vinegar

½ teaspoon sugar

¼ teaspoon soy sauce

½ teaspoon Dijon mustard

½ teaspoon sweet paprika

1 drop Tabasco

1 medium head radicchio, about the size of a small grapefruit

½ head chopped romaine lettuce

One 6-ounce (175 g) Grilled Chicken Breast (page 29), sliced into bite-sized pieces

½ avocado, diced

1 small tomato, diced (about ¼ cup)

¼ cup thinly sliced red onions

½ cup crumbled Maytag blue cheese

3 strips bacon, cooked crisp and crumbled

¼ cup grated carrot, about half of a carrot

Freshly ground black pepper

Makes 2 to 3 servings as an entrée

The Sattvic
Baby lettuce with a citrus peppercorn dressing

I try to do yoga for 20 minutes every morning as it relieves stress, maintains flexibility, builds my confidence, and promotes overall wellness. Yoga can also be part of a lifestyle of eating pure, good foods, called *sattvic*. Sattvic foods are judged by the quality of their life force (prana) and the affect they have on consciousness. I like to get good prana and raise my level of consciousness all at once in one terrific salad. Spring baby greens have a great life force. They are particularly refreshing with almonds and cantaloupe. Pair this salad with vegetarian pizzas such as the creamy and spicy Asparago (page 102), or the earthy Aristan (page 105).

To save time: Make this dressing up to 3 days in advance.

1 Place the Citrus Peppercorn Dressing ingredients a small bowl and mix well. Chill for 15 minutes to let the flavors come together.

2 Meanwhile, fill a large bowl or Bakery Bowl (page 140) with the baby lettuce. Sprinkle the remaining ingredients on top. Pour the Citrus Peppercorn Dressing over all, garnish with the cantaloupe, and serve.

INGREDIENTS

Citrus Peppercorn Dressing

1 teaspoon orange zest

3 tablespoons freshly squeezed orange juice

1 tablespoon lemon juice

1 teaspoon lemon zest

2 tablespoons honey

1 teaspoon soy sauce

1 teaspoon sesame oil

½ teaspoon freshly ground black pepper

3 cups baby lettuce (spring mix)

1 small tomato, diced, about ¼ cup

¼ cup dried cranberries

¼ cup sliced almonds

1 cup shredded carrots, about 1 large carrot

1 tablespoon fresh mint leaves, torn

Garnish

4 to 6 slices cantaloupe, 2 per plate

Makes 2 to 3 servings as a side salad

Voodoo Passion Shrimp Salad

Blackened shrimp with tropical fruit vinaigrette

When I first met Karla, I was working as a chef at the Westin Hotel in Atlanta, Georgia, where she was a waitress. To woo her, I sent her a special meal each day. This entrée salad is the one that made her fall for me: spicy blackened shrimp laced with a sweet, tangy tropical fruit vinaigrette. If you come across fresh passion fruit, buy two. Cut it in half and squeeze it into a bowl with a strainer over it to catch the seeds. Add 1 teaspoon sugar to the vinaigrette. Serve with the Frommagian (page 107), the classic Margheritan (page 110), or the Asparago (page 102).

To save time: Make the dressing up to 3 days ahead.

1 To make the Tropical Fruit Vinaigrette, bring the juice to a boil in a wide skillet. Simmer on low until syrupy and reduced to ¼ cup, about 20 minutes. Cool for 10 minutes.

2 Pour the syrup into a blender. Add the remaining ingredients and blend for about 30 seconds. Chill for 15 minutes to let the flavors come together.

3 Meanwhile, rinse the shrimp under cold running water and pat dry with a paper towel. Toss the shrimp with the blackening spice in a medium bowl, coating them completely. Heat a medium cast-iron skillet, or regular sauté pan (do not use nonstick), on high until very hot, about 5 minutes. Turn on the exhaust fan. Add the Herbed Grill Oil. Add the shrimp and sear on one side until blackened, about 2 minutes. Turn them over and take the skillet off the heat. Do not overcook the shrimp.

4 Toss the lettuce and red cabbage with half the Tropical Fruit Vinaigrette in a large bowl. Top with the remaining ingredients. Place the blackened shrimp on top of the salad. Spoon the reserved vinaigrette over them and serve.

INGREDIENTS

Tropical Fruit Vinaigrette

1 cup sweetened passion fruit juice (or guava or pineapple juice)

¼ cup extra virgin olive oil

2 tablespoons honey

2 tablespoons apple cider vinegar

1 teaspoon lemon juice

1 teaspoon lemon zest

⅛ teaspoon salt

12 large shrimp, peeled and deveined, patted dry

2 tablespoons blackening spice (such as Paul Prudhomme's boxed blackening spice mix)

1 tablespoon Herbed Grill Oil (page 28) or extra virgin olive oil

3 cups chopped romaine lettuce

½ cup chopped red cabbage

½ cup shredded sharp Cheddar

¼ cup thinly sliced red onions

½ jalapeño pepper, seeded and diced (see Note)

Note: When working with hot peppers such as jalapeños, do not touch your eyes. Wash your hands, utensils, and cutting board thoroughly as soon as you are finished.

Makes 2 to 3 servings as an entrée

When I plan a meal I start at dessert and work backwards. No matter how good a meal is, even while people are in the middle of eating, they contemplate what's coming for dessert. Here's your chance to keep the fun going by serving another pizza or piadina for dessert. I bet your guests have never had anything like them. They showcase toppings such as grilled fruit, liqueurs, rich cheese, caramel sauce, and of course, chocolate.

Desserts

The Apple Tart
Apples with a cinnamon glaze

Inspired by the French chef's ability to turn just a few simple ingredients into a mouthwatering dish, this simple dessert pizza features sliced apples that rest on a buttery crust. It looks like a French tart, with a cinnamon glaze to keep the apples warm. I like to use Fuji or Gala apples because they stay firm when cooked.

1 Mix the cinnamon and sugar in a small bowl. Brush the crust with the melted butter. Sprinkle with half of the cinnamon sugar.

2 Lay the apple slices over the pizza, then sprinkle the remaining cinnamon sugar on top.

3 Grill the pizza according to Chapter 4. Before serving, broil it in the oven for up to two minutes, to brown the apples and caramelize the sugar. Watch it closely to avoid burning. Let it cool for a few minutes before cutting. Sprinkle with the slivered almonds, if desired.

INGREDIENTS

2 teaspoons cinnamon

½ cup sugar

1 grilled pizza crust

2 tablespoons unsalted butter, melted

2 medium red apples, cored, halved, and thinly sliced

Garnish (optional)

¼ cup slivered almonds

Makes one 12-inch (30 cm) pizza

Grilled Banana Split

Blackened banana with pizza sugar cookies

Grilled bananas are a popular street snack in Thailand. Venders put whole bananas on the grill and cook them until the skin turns dark and the inside softens. The flavor deepens and intensifies. A simple brown sugar sauce tops these flavorful bananas. Add a little ice cream and some pizza sugar cookies, and you've got a sophisticated dessert.

1 To make the Brown Sugar Sauce, place the apple juice and cornstarch in a small saucepan and stir until well mixed. Place the saucepan over medium heat and add the brown sugar, butter, vanilla, and salt. Stir, allowing the sauce to come to a boil. Cook for about 5 minutes, until it becomes syrupy. Turn the heat to low to keep the syrup warm, or reheat before serving.

2 Brush the pizza crust generously on both sides with the melted butter, then break it into large cookie-sized pieces. Pour the sugar in a large bag, put the crust pieces in the bag, and shake gently. The crust pieces should be completely coated in sugar.

3 Place the whole bananas, still in the peel, on the grill. They should blacken on one side in about 5 minutes. Turn them over and grill for another 5 minutes, until they are black and soft. If they begin to split open, take them off the grill.

4 Put each banana on a plate or in a banana-split dish. Slit them open and pull the peel apart to reveal the soft, steaming banana. Place three little scoops of ice cream alongside the banana and spoon some of the brown sugar sauce over all. Place a couple of pizza cookies next to the banana and serve.

INGREDIENTS

Brown Sugar Sauce

¼ cup apple juice

½ teaspoon cornstarch

½ cup brown sugar

2 tablespoons unsalted butter

1 teaspoon vanilla extract

Pinch of salt

1 pizza crust, grilled on both sides

2 tablespoons melted butter

½ cup sugar

3 ripe whole bananas, unpeeled

9 small scoops of vanilla ice cream

Makes 3 servings

Cinnamon Churros
Sugary crusts with ice cream and syrup

In Spain and Mexico, street vendors sell irresistible sugary donuts called *churros*. For this dessert, I dip hot crusts in cinnamon and sugar like *churros,* then fold them into little sandwiches filled with ice cream and topped with chocolate syrup. You might tell yourself these are only for the kids but I've yet to see an adult resist them.

1 Combine the cinnamon and sugar in a medium bowl.

2 Roll the pieces of dough into small crusts about 4 inches (10 cm) wide. Grill them according to Chapter 4, but grill the other side for a minute as well.

3 Brush both sides of the crust with melted butter. Place the crust in the bowl of cinnamon sugar and coat well.

4 Place two crusts on each serving plate. Put a small scoop of ice cream in each crust. Fold the sandwich in half and press down to seal. Drizzle the chocolate syrup over all and serve.

INGREDIENTS

½ teaspoon cinnamon

3 tablespoons sugar

½ recipe pizza dough (see page 22), cut into 6 equal pieces

2 tablespoons melted butter

6 mini scoops of ice cream

2 to 3 tablespoons chocolate syrup

Makes 6 folded sandwiches, serves 3

Grasshopper Pie
Marshmallow, chocolate, and Crème de Menthe

Before I was old enough to drink, I watched my dad mix up a green concoction in a blender and pour it into highball glasses. I begged him for a taste, only because I loved its emerald color. He said it was a Grasshopper. It was cool and minty with a hint of white chocolate and cream. Grasshoppers get their color from Crème de Menthe. I've used it in this dessert pizza, combined with marshmallow and an Oreo crumb crust, for a minty chocolate flavor.

1 Put the chocolate chips in a small microwaveable bowl. Heat for 30 seconds to melt the chips, then stir. If they are not melted completely, repeat for 15 seconds at a time until the chocolate chips melt into a thick sauce. Stir in the sweetened condensed milk until the chocolate thickens.

2 Spoon the marshmallow cream into a small bowl. Add 2 tablespoons of the Crème de Menthe and mix well. It will turn a pretty shade of green.

3 Put 8 Oreos in a thick plastic bag with a sealable top. Crush the cookies with a rolling pin until they turn to fine crumbs.

4 Brush the grilled side of the pizza crust with the melted butter. Sprinkle the cookie crumbs over the top, and add small dollops of the chocolate fudge without spreading it. Next add small dollops of the green marshmallow cream. The pizza should look checkered, with alternating dollops of chocolate and green. Break up the remaining Oreos into ½-inch (12 mm) pieces and scatter them across the pizza.

5 Grill the pizza according to Chapter 4. Drizzle the remaining 2 tablespoons of Crème de Menthe over the pizza and serve.

INGREDIENTS

⅓ cup semisweet chocolate chips

⅓ cup sweetened condensed milk

One 7-ounce (200 g) jar prepared marshmallow cream

4 tablespoons crème de Menthe

12 Oreo cookies

1 grilled pizza crust

1 tablespoon melted unsalted butter

Makes one 12-inch (30 cm) pizza

Grilled Pears Saint André

Pears, creamy cheese, and spiced sugar

Saint André is a soft, ripe triple-cream cheese similar to Brie and Camembert, but even more rich. It melts between the grilled pears like butter. Sugar and a bit of nutmeg give this pizza its sweetness and spice. Choose Bartlett or Comice pears and let them ripen on your counter. Bosc pears are harder and take longer to roast.

1 Pour the olive oil and lemon juice into a large bowl. Add the pear slices and toss to coat completely.

2 Prepare a medium hot grill with the coals pushed to one side. Place the pears on the indirect side so that they cook slowly, without burning. Grill for about 5 minutes on each side, until slightly soft.

3 Mix the sugar and nutmeg together in a small bowl. Brush the grilled side of the pizza crust with the melted butter. Sprinkle half the spiced sugar on top.

4 Cut the rind off of the Saint André and discard. Cut the cheese into 1-inch (2½ cm) cubes and scatter them over the sugared crust. Top with the grilled pears and the remaining spiced sugar.

5 Grill the pizza according to Chapter 4. Sprinkle with the chopped mint, if desired, and serve.

INGREDIENTS

1 tablespoon extra virgin olive oil

1 tablespoon lemon juice

2 medium ripe pears, quartered, cored, and thinly sliced

⅓ cup sugar

¼ teaspoon nutmeg

1 grilled pizza crust

1 tablespoon unsalted butter, melted

6 to 7 ounces (175 to 200 g) Saint André or other mild triple-cream cheese

Garnish (optional)

1 tablespoon chopped fresh mint

Makes one 12-inch (30 cm) pizza

The S'more
Graham crackers, chocolate, and marshmallow

One summer night I was grilling pizza over a big campfire in my backyard. I realized that in my pantry I had all the makings for S'mores, the classic campfire dessert of graham crackers, melted chocolate, and caramelized marshmallows. I put the components together for this S'more pizza, and my kids went wild. A graham cracker crust goes right on top of the crisp pizza crust. Then it's piled with hot fudge and gooey marshmallow cream, sold at most grocery stores. Everyone will want s'more.

1 Put the chocolate chips in a small microwaveable bowl. Heat for 30 seconds to melt the chips, then stir. If they are not melted completely, repeat for 15 seconds at a time until the chocolate chips melt into a thick sauce. Stir in the sweetened condensed milk until the chocolate thickens.

2 Place 7 of the graham crackers in a thick plastic bag with a sealable top. Crush the crackers with a rolling pin until they become fine crumbs.

3 Brush the grilled side of the pizza crust with the melted butter. Pour the graham cracker crumbs over the buttered crust, smoothing them evenly over the crust with your hand. Add small dollops of the chocolate fudge without spreading. Do the same with the marshmallow cream. The pizza should look checkered, with alternating dollops of chocolate and cream. Break the two remaining graham crackers into 1-inch (2½ cm) pieces and scatter them across the pizza.

4 Grill the pizza according to Chapter 4. Before serving, broil it in the oven for up to two minutes, to brown the marshmallow. Watch it closely to avoid burning.

INGREDIENTS

½ cup semisweet chocolate chips

½ cup sweetened condensed milk

9 full graham crackers (1 package)

1 grilled pizza crust

2 tablespoons melted unsalted butter

One 7-ounce (200 g) jar prepared marshmallow cream

Makes one 12-inch (30 cm) pizza

Dessert Piadina Dough
Soft buttery crust

I created this tender dough especially for dessert piadinas. It's softer than regular piadina dough and more like a biscuit, with a rich, buttery flavor. Of course, you can use the traditional piadina dough for desserts as well. Dessert piadinas are smaller than regular piadinas. The volume of this recipe can be doubled easily.

1 **Kneading with a stand mixer:** Add the flour, salt, and sugar to a 4- or 5-quart (4- or 5-liter) mixing bowl. Use the dough hook attachment on the lowest speed to combine the dry ingredients. Make a well in the center. Pour the warm water, lemon juice, and melted butter into the center and stir slowly until the dough becomes too thick to stir. Knead for 5 minutes at medium speed.

   Kneading with a food processor: Use the plastic blade made especially for dough as the metal blade can tear the dough to pieces. Put the flour, salt, and sugar in the food processor. Pulse to combine. Add the warm water, lemon juice, and melted butter. Use a pulse action until the dough comes together. Continue to pulse the dough in quick bursts for about 3 minutes. This technique keeps the dough from overheating.

   Kneading by hand: Put the flour, salt, and sugar in a large mixing bowl. Stir to combine the ingredients. Make a well in the center. Pour the warm water, lemon juice, and melted butter into the center and stir slowly until the dough comes together. Lightly flour a clean, dry countertop. Form a ball of dough and place it on the counter. Press down with the palm of your hand. Fold the dough over itself and press again. Continue to roll and press the dough. Knead for about 8 minutes, until the dough is smooth. You will feel it change as it softens and becomes more elastic. Add only enough flour to prevent it from sticking.

2 The dough should be soft and smooth. Put the olive oil in a medium
bowl. Add the dough and turn it over several times until it is covered
in oil. Wrap in plastic and let it rest for 30 minutes.

3 Place the dough on a floured countertop and cut it into 4 equal
pieces. Use a rolling pin to flatten the pieces into 8-inch (20 cm)
rounds. Follow the Piadina Grilling Steps (pages 120–121) to finish.

Piadina Rösti
Roasted pears, mascarpone, and honey

In fall, pears are at their peak of flavor. It's the best time to make this luscious dessert of pears roasted with butter and honey. Roasting fruit makes it tender and deepens the flavor. When combined with rich, buttery mascarpone, it brings the flavor of Italy's countryside to your plate. Choose Bartlett or Comice pears and let them ripen on your counter. Bosc pears are harder and take longer to roast.

To save time: Make the roasted fruit up to 3 days in advance.

1 Preheat the oven to 350°F (180°C). Place the fruit in a 12 x 9 x 2 inch (30 x 11½ x 5 cm) dish.

2 Melt the butter in a small microwaveable bowl. Add the honey, sugar, lemon zest, lemon juice, and flour and mix well. Pour over the fruit and toss to coat.

3 Roast for 1 hour, until the fruit is soft enough to be cut with a fork. The syrup should be thick and brown. Stir occasionally during the roasting and baste with the syrup.

4 Combine the mascarpone, powdered sugar, and vanilla in a small bowl.

5 Lightly brush the hot dessert piadina rounds with the tablespoon of melted butter. Place each piadina on a dessert plate. Spoon the mascarpone into the center, and add some of the fruit and syrup. Fold in half, drizzle some syrup on top, garnish with the lemon zest curls, and serve.

INGREDIENTS

2 medium ripe pears, cored, halved, and thinly sliced

1 tablespoon unsalted butter, plus 1 tablespoon for brushing

4 tablespoons honey

1 tablespoon sugar

Zest of ½ lemon

1 teaspoon lemon juice

½ teaspoon flour

4 ounces (100 g) mascarpone, at room temperature

1 tablespoon powdered sugar

¼ teaspoon vanilla extract

1 recipe Dessert Piadina Dough (page 168)

Garnish
A few curls of lemon zest

Makes 4 dessert piadinas

Piadina Limone
Lemon curd with blueberries and cream

The first time I made this lemon curd and blueberry piadina, I served it to my boss, Lester Crown. This man travels the globe, dining in the world's finest restaurants, yet he said, "Craig, that was extraordinary!" It is rare to get this kind of a response from him. I knew I had a winner.

1 Fill a large pot about a third full of water. Bring it to a boil and turn it down to a simmer. Place the eggs, lemon juice, lemon zest, and sugar in a stainless-steel or glass bowl large enough to fit over the top of the open pot. Place the bowl on the pot, high enough so that the water does not touch it.

2 Whip the sauce with a wire whisk until it becomes thick like sour cream, about 8 minutes.

3 Cut the butter into pieces and whip them into the curd, one at a time, until each piece is fully incorporated. Refrigerate, covered, for at least 1 hour. The curd will thicken as it chills.

4 Place each grilled piadina round on a dessert plate. Spoon the lemon curd onto one half of each. Follow with the whipped cream and blueberries, and top with the crushed cookies. Fold each piadina in half, dust with powdered sugar, and serve.

INGREDIENTS

Lemon Curd

2 large eggs, plus 1 egg yolk

3 tablespoons fresh lemon juice (do not use bottled lemon juice)

½ tablespoon finely shredded lemon zest

6 tablespoons sugar

4 tablespoons unsalted butter, at room temperature

1 recipe Dessert Piadina Dough (page 168)

½ cup heavy cream, whipped stiff

1 cup fresh blueberries

2 ounces (50 g) shortbread cookies (about 6 small cookies), crushed

Powdered sugar for dusting

Makes 4 dessert piadinas

Piadina Caramelata
Chocolate fudge with caramel sauce

As a kid, I raced my bike down to the candy store almost every day to get Marathon Bars, those long caramel and chocolate candy bars. As an adult, I still love those flavors, but I've learned that the best caramel is made from scratch. It only takes about 6 minutes, so there is no excuse for not trying your hand. This piadina is named after two Italian words: *caramel*, which is exactly the same as our English word; and *cioccolata*, meaning chocolate. Come prepared with a sweet tooth for my favorite dessert piadina.

1   To prepare the Caramel Sauce, melt the butter in a large, heavy saucepan on low heat. Add the sugar and salt and stir until dissolved. Increase to medium heat and boil the sauce for 3 minutes, stirring occasionally. The sauce will turn a reddish brown. Turn the heat to low and let it cool down for a few minutes.

2   Stir in the cream, being careful not to burn yourself, as the sauce will bubble up. Continue to simmer, stirring constantly for 3 minutes. Remove from the heat, and let cool slightly.

3   Meanwhile, to prepare the fudge, place the chocolate chips in a medium microwave-safe bowl and microwave on high for 30 seconds, then stir. If the chips are not melted, microwave for another 15 seconds. Repeat until melted. Be careful not to overheat them or they will burn.

4   Place each grilled piadina round on a dessert plate. Spoon some of the chocolate fudge onto one half of each. Follow with similar amounts of marshmallow cream and warm caramel sauce. Fold each piadina in half and drizzle with a little more caramel sauce. Add a scoop of vanilla ice cream, if desired, and serve.

INGREDIENTS

Caramel Sauce

2 tablespoons unsalted butter

¼ cup brown sugar

Pinch of salt

¼ cup heavy cream

¼ cup semisweet chocolate chips

¼ cup sweetened condensed milk

One 7-ounce (200 g) jar prepared marshmallow cream

1 recipe Dessert Piadina Dough (page 168)

Vanilla ice cream, optional

Makes 4 dessert piadinas

Piadina Torrone
Homemade nougat and caramel sauce

Italian nougat, a chewy candy of sugared egg whites and toasted nuts, is labor intensive to prepare. After experimenting, I devised an easy and foolproof way to make this soft confection at home, using high-quality white chocolate (made with cocoa butter instead of hydrogenated oils) and marshmallow cream, available at most grocery stores. This recipe is assembled quickly and served warm, with the piadina grilled at the last minute. It's rich, gooey, and sweet, with a little salt and crunch from the pecans.

1 Place the white chocolate chips in a medium microwave-safe bowl and microwave on high for 30 seconds, then stir. If the chips are not melted, microwave for another 15 seconds. Repeat until melted. Be careful not to overheat them or they will burn.

2 Stir the marshmallow cream into the white chocolate. Add the toasted nuts and the dried cranberries and stir. The nougat will thicken and become hard to stir like taffy. If the nougat cools, it will harden. Microwave on high for 5 seconds to soften.

3 Lightly brush the hot piadina rounds with the melted butter. Place each round on a dessert plate. Place a large spoonful of nougat on one side of each, and spoon the warm caramel sauce over the nougat. Fold each piadina in half. Sprinkle with powdered sugar and serve.

INGREDIENTS

½ cup white chocolate chips

1½ cups marshmallow cream

¼ cup chopped pecan pieces, toasted (see page 29)

2 tablespoons dried cranberries

1 recipe Dessert Piadina Dough (page 168)

1 tablespoon melted butter

¼ cup Caramel Sauce (page 174), warmed

Powdered sugar for dusting

Makes 4 dessert piadinas

After many years of catering grilled pizza events, I can pass on helpful information to guide you on throwing a fun and unique party. I've included four sample menus with accompanying grocery lists, as well as suggestions of what kinds of drinks to serve. You'll plan a menu, shop, work ahead, and create a game plan for success. Guests will talk about your party for days afterward. Just turn the page to get started.

Party
Planning

Party Planning Steps

When I throw a grilled pizza party, I serve great cocktails, crank up the tunes, and inevitably, everyone ends up crowding around the grill to watch the action. It makes the party more like an event, and best of all, it makes people happy. Now it's your turn. First, you'll want to feel confident. To eliminate any apprehension about grilling in front of friends, make the intended pizzas or piadinas beforehand so you'll know what to expect. Then when grilled pizza voyeurs watch as you slide the pizzas across the grill, you'll enjoy the experience as much as they do.

Scope your ingredients

If you choose one of the menus in this chapter, you'll be ahead of the game. If you want to create your own menu, look at ingredients you already have on hand. There's only one cup of cantaloupe in the Emilian's Cantaloupe Chutney, for example. All the chicken pizzas can be made with a handful of leftover cooked chicken. So when you are staring into your icebox, remember how existing ingredients can be turned into a grilled pizza and piadina party.

Use the same ingredients in different ways to get more mileage from your grocery money. Tomatoes can go in a salad as well as in a piadina. Grilled chicken appears on the Thai Peanut Pong Gari and the Texan without guests thinking they're eating the same pizza.

Balance your workload

Some pizzas have more prep work than others. Pair an elaborate pizza with a simpler one. If both selections are complex, you can overwhelm the palate as well as yourself. Sometimes the simplest pizzas are the ones that stand out.

Write down your menu

It is the best way to begin any cooking project, because from this menu comes a prep list of all the sauces, chutneys, and other toppings to make in advance.

Work ahead

Use the examples I give in this chapter to help you figure out your own schedule. By working just a little each day on tasks that can be done in advance, you'll be comfortable just grillin' and chillin' the actual day of your party.

KITCHEN STAPLES

The grocery lists for these menus do not include the following staples. Please check your cupboards and refrigerator before heading out.

- flour
- cornmeal
- yeast
- sugar
- extra virgin olive oil
- mayonnaise
- unsalted butter
- eggs
- dried oregano
- dried thyme
- dried basil
- cinnamon
- salt
- freshly ground black pepper
- fresh garlic

**HEAD COUNT AND
RECIPE YIELDS**

When figuring out how many pizzas and
piadinas to make for a party, multiply any
recipe to achieve the correct amount of food
per person. Whether you're planning a party of
10 guests or 100, plan on two people per 12-
inch (30 cm) pizza, or 1½ piadinas per person.
Usually I cut the piadinas in half.

Create a shopping list

Lump all the produce and meat ingredients
together, so you don't have to run back to that
section of the market several times. Check
your cupboards to make sure you have the
staples on hand. If you prefer, buy the pre-
made ingredients suggested in some recipes.

Get a helper

Being a professional chef, I'm used to
working alone, but you might not be. Advance
coordination with others can help a lot on
party day. Plus, it's more fun to work on a
party with friends. A helper who likes to cook
can go over the details in advance and give
feedback on how to streamline the work. It
might work best, for example, to have one
person at the grill and one person putting
ingredients on the pizza, or finishing them
under the broiler.

Review, review, review

Usually the details that are not written down
are the ones that come back to bite you. Do
your best to think of everything.

The Southern Italian Party

While northern Italians enjoy butter and cream sauces, southern Italians base more dishes on the tomato. Here's a grilled pizza party based on the southern Italian cuisine found from Naples through Sicily and Palermo. Southerners love a great feast and social gatherings. Traditionally, the women work together in the kitchen, particularly on making the dough.

The Menu

Pizzas: The Margheritan (page 110) and the Vesuvian (page 83)
Salad: Escarole Siciliano (page 145)
Dessert: Piadina Caramelata (page 174)
Beverage: A fruity wine, such as Chianti

Three days before

- Go shopping, starting with the grocery list on the opposite page. Fill in the specific amounts you'll need of each ingredient, based on the number of servings.

Two days before

- Make the dough and refrigerate
- Prepare the caramel sauce

The day before

- Roll out the dough and grill the crusts
- Make the Chunky Tomato Basil Sauce (page 28)
- Slice and cook the potatoes

A few hours before

- Grill the chicken
- Slice the onions and tomatoes

- Wash and tear the escarole and refrigerate
- Prepare the fudge
- Make the piadina using extra pizza dough (or make piadina dough)

An hour before eating

- Light the grill. You need half an hour to get the charcoal going, then another 10 minutes or so to cool it a little. If you're grilling indoors, heat the grill or pan at least 10 minutes before. The worst thing is to have guests standing around waiting for a fire. I'd rather have the fire burn up a little and have to add some more coals than not have a good strong fire.
- Get your ingredients ready in little bowls, grouped by pizza
- Build your pizzas

When the grill is ready

- Grill the pizzas
- Heat the caramel and fudge sauces in the microwave
- Assemble the piadinas
- Toss the salad
- Serve the food buffet style

GROCERIES

Dairy

grated Parmesan

shredded mozzarella

fresh mozzarella

crumbled Asiago

heavy cream

Meat

boneless, skinless chicken breasts

Prepared foods

Italian dressing

tomato paste

black olives

brown sugar

semisweet chocolate chips

marshmallow cream

sweetened condensed milk

Produce

potatoes

tomatoes

red onions

escarole

lemons

fresh Italian parsley

fresh basil

GROCERIES

Dairy

shredded Parmesan

shredded mozzarella

fresh mozzarella

white Cheddar

crumbled feta

Meat

pepperoni

Prepared foods

tomato paste

graham crackers

semisweet chocolate chips

sweetened condensed milk

marshmallow cream

Produce

tomatoes

fresh basil

fresh Italian parsley

The Kid's Blast Party

Kids love grilled pizzas. I think it's the thin crust. They can eat more slices, and that's always fun. When they first see me grilling pizza, they laugh and wonder how it could be possible. I tell them just about anything is possible—next stop, a trip to the moon! Children are fun to cook with too, because they become intent on doing the jobs you give them. Recruit yours for some of the tasks below.

The Menu

Pizzas: The Margheritan (page 110) with pepperoni and the Fromaggian (page 107)
Dessert: The S'more (page 166)
Beverage: Freshly squeezed lemonade

Three days before

- Go shopping, starting with the grocery list on the opposite page. Fill in the amounts you'll need of each ingredient, based on the number of servings.

Two days before

- Make the dough and refrigerate

The day before

- Roll out the dough and grill the crusts
- Make the Chunky Tomato Basil Sauce (page 28)
- Make the fudge for the S'more, wrap it tightly in plastic wrap, and refrigerate

A few hours before

- Crumble the graham crackers
- Make the lemonade

An hour before eating

- Light the grill. You need half an hour to get the charcoal going, then another 10 minutes or so to cool it a little.
- Melt the butter
- Get your ingredients ready in little bowls, grouped by pizza type
- Build your pizzas

When the grill is ready

- Grill the pizzas
- Serve the lemonade
- Serve the food buffet style

The Elegant Cocktail Party

Does pizza really belong at a cocktail party? You bet. I've served grilled pizzas at the most upscale affairs in very ritzy homes. People smell them grilling and anticipate something unusual. When they see the pizzas on a platter they get excited. When they take a bite, they are all yours. I cut the pieces a little smaller so that they can be eaten in two bites. That way each piece of pizza becomes a fancy canapé.

The Menu
Pizzas: The Gamberian (page 95) and the Parma e Fiche (page 60)
Salad: The Grapefruit Caesar (page 148)
Dessert: The Apple Tart (page 158)
Beverage: Champagne

Up to three months ahead
- Make the pesto and freeze

Three days before
- Go shopping, starting with the grocery list on the opposite page. Fill in the amounts you'll need of each ingredient, based on the number of servings.

Two days before
- Make the dough and refrigerate

The day before
- Roll out the dough and grill the crust
- Make the Chunky Tomato Basil Sauce (page 28)
- Make the Caesar dressing
- Make the fig sauce
- Cook the shrimp and refrigerate

A few hours before
- Prepare the lettuce for the salad
- Cut the apples, place them in a bowl, and toss with lemon juice to prevent darkening. Cover with plastic wrap.
- Make the cinnamon sugar
- Melt the butter

An hour before eating
- Light the grill. You need half an hour to get the charcoal going, then another 10 minutes or so to cool it a little.
- Get your ingredients ready in little bowls, grouped by pizza
- Build your pizzas

When the grill is ready
- Serve the champagne
- Grill the pizzas
- Serve the food buffet style

GROCERIES

Dairy

grated Parmesan

shredded Mozzarella

crumbled Gorgonzola

Fontina

Meat and Seafood

jumbo shrimp

prosciutto

Prepared foods

sun-dried tomatoes

pesto sauce (if you're not making it)

capers

apple juice

brown sugar

tomato paste

red vinegar

Dijon mustard

Worcestershire sauce

slivered almonds

Produce

figs

red onions

tomatoes

pecans

Jonathan, Fuji, or Gala apples

lemons

romaine lettuce

red grapefruit

fresh basil

fresh Italian parsley

The All Piadina Party

Sometimes a party calls for sandwiches. Impress your guests by serving piadinas instead of the usual sandwich fare. These Italian sandwich wraps are all about simplicity, elegance, and great taste. Platters of piadinas, cut into halves for just the right size per serving, look beautiful. Make plenty because they always go fast. A side salad completes your meal, along with a sweet piadina for a luscious finish.

The Menu

Piadinas: The Firenze (page 125), the Genovese (page 126), and the Mortadella (page 129)
Salad: The Greek (page 149)
Dessert: The Limone (page 172)
Beverage: Lager or pale ale

Up to three months before

- Make the pesto sauce and freeze it

Three days before

- Go shopping, starting with the grocery list on the opposite page. Fill in the amounts you'll need of each ingredient, based on the number of servings.

Two days before

- Make the piadina dough, wrap, and refrigerate
- Make the lemon curd

The day before

- Make the Greek dressing
- Cut the cucumbers, red peppers, and onions
- Roll out the piadina dough and grill, then wrap up tightly and refrigerate

A few hours before

- Assemble the Greek salad, but do not dress
- Whip the heavy cream
- Crumble the shortbread cookies
- Grill the eggplant slices and red peppers
- Bring the piadinas to room temperature
- Grill the chicken breast
- Get your ingredients ready in little bowls, grouped by piadina

An hour before the party

- Assemble the Piadina Firenze and the Genovese
- Assemble the Piadina Mortadella, but keep the olive relish on the side until it's time to serve.
- Cut the piadinas into halves and place on trays
- Dress the salad
- Assemble the Piadina Limone

During the party

- Serve the food buffet style

GROCERIES

Dairy

Parmesan

crumbled feta

heavy cream

Meat, chicken, fish, and eggs

boneless skinless chicken breast

anchovies

mortadella

Prepared foods

balsamic and red wine vinegar

Kalamata and/or green olives

pesto (if you don't make your own)

pepperoncini peppers

shortbread cookies

lemon curd (if you don't make your own)

powdered sugar

pecans

pine nuts

walnuts

Produce

eggplant

tomatoes

red peppers

romaine lettuce

lemons

red onions

yellow onions

celery

cucumbers

blueberries

fresh basil and Italian parsley

Index

Acknowledgments

We are grateful for the support of Henry Crown & Co., particularly Steve Crown. He always has an open door and responds to ideas with enthusiasm and grace. Without the generosity of the Crown family, this book would not be possible.

Thanks to our agent, Carole Bidnick, for her guidance, support, resourcefulness, and eagerness, particularly once she tasted the pizzas and piadinas.

The professionals at DK Publishing could not have done a better job. A big thanks goes to our unflappable editor, Anja Schmidt, always on the same page. She and assistant editor Nicole Morford made skillful edits to strengthen the book's text. Art director Dirk Kaufman designed a gorgeous jacket and interior, showcasing this publisher's prowess in visual art. The hardworking team of photographer Charles Schiller, food stylist Susan Vajaranant, and prop stylist Pamela Duncan Silver created the exquisite photos of food and techniques. We also thank proofreader Ann Cahn and indexer Nanette Cardon.

Thanks to Gretchen Jordan and Maggie Boone for their assistance.

Individually:

Craig: Special thanks to my wife Karla, with whom I have shared many wild grilled pizza adventures. If I didn't meet her, I probably would have never grilled a pizza in the first place. Jerry Kleiner and Marissa Molinaro responded to my pizzas with great enthusiasm early on and sparked my determination to write this book. I'm also thankful for my two beautiful children, Chapel and Kastle, who were born eating grilled pizza with crawdads and other weird things and have always loved their chef daddy.

Dianne: My talented pool of recipe testers and samplers, particularly my husband Owen, helped grill and eat months of pizzas and piadinas. Nani Steele's expertise made her a dream helper and tester in my kitchen. Mary-Margaret Pack good-naturedly tested recipes, thus pleasing her husband, who adores pizza. Gourmet cooks Howard Baldwin and Paula Rheinman tested recipes and provided valuable feedback. Keith Criss helped in the kitchen. Tasters Laura Rubin, Eva and Paul Heninwolf, and Jennifer Lee made constructive comments at the table. Thanks also to cookbook author Greg Patent for sharing his expertise.

Lastly, we'd like to thank all the people behind the scenes, who helped make this book a success.